Darkness at Dachau

The True Story of Father Jean Bernard

Paul F. Caranci

First Stillwater River Publications Edition
ISBN: 978-1-955123-41-9
1 2 3 4 5 6 7 8 9 10
Written by Paul F. Caranci
Front-cover art by Kathy Anzeveno
Back cover image by Scott Beale / Laughing Squid laughingsquid.com
Published by Stillwater River Publications,
Pawtucket, RI, USA.
Publisher's Cataloging-In-Publication Data
(Prepared by The Donohue Group, Inc.)
Publisher's Cataloging-In-Publication Data
(Prepared by The Donohue Group, Inc.)

Names: Caranci, Paul F., author.
Title: Darkness at Dachau : the true story of Father Jean Bernard / Paul F.
Caranci.
Description: First Stillwater River Publications edition. | Pawtucket, RI,
USA : Stillwater River Publications, [2021]
Identifiers: ISBN 9781955123419
Subjects: LCSH: Bernard, Jean, 1907-1994. | Catholic Church--Clergy--
Biography. | Dachau (Concentration camp)--History. | Catholic Church--
Germany--History--1933-1945. | LCGFT: Biographies.
Classification: LCC BX4705.B46 C37 2021 | DDC 940.53/18092 B--dc23
The views and opinions expressed
in this book are solely those of the author
and do not necessarily reflect the views
and opinions of the publisher.

Dedication

Writing books such as this one tends to ground a person and provide a new perspective and a deeper appreciation of the important things in life. Faith, family, friends, and the freedom to enjoy them, are certainly priorities in my life today.

I dedicate this book to my family, my friends, and to this wonderful country that provides my freedom. Above all else, this work is dedicated to God Almighty, without whom none of the aforementioned treasures would have meaning.

Table of Contents

Preface

I t's hard to believe that one human being could be so heartless toward another, deaf to his pleadings, unmoved by his sufferings and gleeful in the administration of his torture. The SS men of Adolf Hitler's Third Reich, however, were selected for possessing those very qualities. The heart-wrenching torture that they administered at the expense of their prisoners; men, women and children who were guilty of nothing more than being born, is hard to understand and even harder to read about. People of various stripes: Jews; Communists, Gypsies, Poles, Religious, asocials, and other people simply living their normal lives, were taken, gathered, imprisoned, tortured, and killed, all for the sake of a one individual's misguided and evil lust for power.

One of the insufficiently discussed targets of Hitler in his quest for world domination, the elimination of religion, the genocide of the Jews, and his plan to create an Aryan nation, were the Catholics and in particular, the Catholic clergy. Hitler had a disdain for all religion. He saw the practice of faith as a weakness and a character flaw that detracted from one's commitment to the Reich. He enlisted men, ruthless men, to ensure that all traces of religious activity would be stricken from his "new world." These men fabricated reasons to arrest and torture as many of these "societal outcasts" as possible hoping to eliminate them from the world. They nearly succeeded.

While this book glimpses the horrors of Germany's war and its effect on Catholicism through the eyes of a Catholic priest, in a much broader sense it explores the depravity of those who would mistreat their fellow human beings so atrociously and explores the effect that such treatment had on those targeted by the evildoers. It is difficult to imagine anyone committing such horrible acts against another person, but it is eye-opening to see just how far a madman can push a compliant society; one that does not question authority, but rather comports to its every demand.

Darkness at Dachau: The True Story of Father Jean Bernard will leave the reader wondering if this blind acquiescence could ever happen again in our world or perhaps whether it already has.

Acknowledgements

I t is with a deep sense of appreciation that I acknowledge the many people who have assisted with the production of this book.

Kathy Anzeveno dedicated a significant amount of time to develop themes that artfully captured the essence of the contents of the tome. That, in and of itself, was no easy task, but Kathy went the extra mile in bringing that theme to life through vivid imagination and the proficient work of her hands.

Doris Brissette has become one of my go-to editors. She has an uncanny talent for detecting and correcting the most minute grammatical error. Her prescient comments reigned in my spurious thoughts, causing me to rewrite several portions of this book many times. I am grateful for her and the time she spent reviewing segments of the manuscript.

Sara Benz, of the North Providence Union Free Library, is always able to locate that hard-to-find book that I typically tend to need in the eleventh hour of my writing, thereby ensuring that all the information I need to complete my work is available to me.

Steven and Dawn Porter, of Stillwater River Publications, who are always ready to assist with all that is necessary to assure a quality publication.

And of course, Margie Caranci, who, despite keeping a full schedule at work, at home, and in the gardens, constantly makes time to listen to me read my chapters aloud with a critical ear that always results in a better finished product.

Finally, I want to thank the staff of the United States Holocaust Memorial Museum in Washington, D.C. and the "American scholars" with whom they connected me. In particular, Jo-Ellyn Decker, the Research and Reference Librarian, Rev. Kevin Spicer at Stonehill College, Dr. James Gregory Chappel at Duke University, and Dr. Michael E. O'Sullivan at Marist University. I am also grateful to the museum for sending me photographs and information and for allowing me to use the images in this book.

Glossary of people, places, and terms important to the story of Dachau

Bernard, Fr. Jean – Prisoner of Dachau from May 19, 1941 to August 6, 1942 and author of *PriestBlock 25487: A Memoir of Dachau.*

Blond Beast – aka BB, the nickname of a ruthless SS officer who was insulted by a remark made by Father Jean Bernard upon his arrival at Dachau.

Brandsma, Fr. Titus – The first clergyman killed at Dachau. He was beatified by Pope John Paul II in 1985.

de Coninck, Fr. Leo – A Belgian priest, superior of the Jesuits in Brussels and professor at the University of Louvain who was arrested and sent to Dachau for offering intellectual resistance to the Third Reich.

Eicke, Theodor – The second commandant of Dachau following the release of Hilmar Wäckerle. Eicke issued regulations for Dachau that became the blueprint for the daily operation of all Nazi camps.

Esch, Dr. Baptiste – A Catholic priest at Dachau also known as "Batty." An editor of the *Luxemburger Wort*. He was transferred to Dachau in early October 1941.

Hayden, Josef – The Chief Capo of Dachau. He was also a madman who performed needless surgeries on prisoners to satisfy his curiosity and lust for blood.

Nuremberg Laws – A series of decrees passed by Hitler supporting the goal of ethnic cleansing.

Schiltz, Fr. – Assigned to room 1 of barrack 28 with Fr. Bernard and Fr. Batty Esch in October 1941.

Schutzstaffel – Known by the nickname SS, they were originally established as Adolf Hitler's personal bodyguard unit, but the SS would later become an elite guard of the Nazi Reich. It also served as Hitler's executive force and was selected to carry out all security-related duties. They operated outside of the constraints of the legal system.

Stoffels, Fr. Joseph – From the Congregation of the Priests of the Sacred Heart in Luxembourg, Stoffels was a long-time friend of Fr. Bernard. He was transferred to Dachau from Buchenwald in October 1941.

Truncheon – A short, hard stick carried and used by the Schutzstaffel (SS) guards and the capos to beat prisoners.

Wäckerle, Hilmar – An SS officer selected as the first commandant of Dachau.

Waffen SS – an elite SS combat unit whose troops also helped run the concentration camps

Wampach, Fr. Nicolas – Another priest from the Congregation of the Priests of the Sacred Heart in Luxembourg, Wampach was a long-time friend of Fr. Bernard. He was transferred to Dachau from Buchenwald in October 1941.

Introduction

Welcome to Dachau

Dachau Prison Camp
May 19, 1941

The encounter was all too surreal and his mind slipped back to a better time. The sights and sounds of the family reunion tickled his senses and the smell emanating from the expensive meats and accoutrements that lined the buffet table caused his mouth to water. He danced to the melodic tunes sung by his mother and sister as his father played the piano with a dexterity reserved for someone worthy of the symphony. Those gathered around him laughed as he performed what may just have been the most poorly choreographed dance steps ever imagined. He joined them in laughter and wiped a bead of sweat from his forehead while taking a few steps toward the buffet table.

Suddenly a sharp blow to his spine abruptly ended the party. A second whack from the truncheon, the short stick carried by the Schutzstaffel (SS) guards and the capos, slashed across his back simultaneously, thrusting him into the consciousness of the here and now. For the past three-and-a-half months, Fr. Jean Bernard had found himself "in police custody, among regular prisoners, but [he had now] entered the special domain of the SS,"[1] and what he experienced personally and witnessed happening to others was truly horrifying.

His personal effects, including his collar, bible, rosary, medals, and all other items that might otherwise have identified him as a Catholic priest, had already been collected in a paper bag and sent to the administration building. The guard was using the sharp point of his truncheon to direct his completely naked prisoner toward the cleansing station. The line of men moved along quickly with particular care taken by neither the prisoners forced into servitude as capos nor the guards who watched with delight the brutality with which the capos exercised their authority. In fact, to some extent, it was the degree of the brutality that allowed the capos to maintain their positions. Capos were prisoners carefully selected by the SS to act as drill sergeants assuring that no prisoner stepped out of line. He was required to enforce the barrack rules with strict authority and certain brutality under the constant risk of falling victim to an even more severe beating from the SS if he failed.

Once within the barrack, Fr. Bernard's cleansing process began. His head was shaved first "by means of rudimentary clippers that tore out the hair"[2] rather than cutting it. The same dull clippers were used to shave his torso from face to pubic area. When adequately cleansed of all hair, including armpit hair, the prisoners were pushed forward where another group of appointed prisoners were "ordered to paint the newcomers with cresol, a powerful disinfectant. On the genital mucus membranes and the areas that had just been shaved, the product caused severe burns that made the men double over in pain."[3] Then the line of agonizing prisoners was shoved into the grand shower room where first freezing, and then scalding water was used to cleanse the body of any clinging hair, cresol or other excrement that may have been released during the excruciatingly painful and humiliating process.

The naked men were issued old ragged clothes consisting of pants, shirts, and jackets of varying sizes. There was no method to the distribution process. Whatever lay on top of the pile was given to the next man in line. Nothing fit, nor did it seem to matter to anyone. "Finally, the prisoners received a mess tin, a spoon and a pair of wooden clogs that would not stay on unless they curled their toes painfully."[4]

The initial dehumanization process was deemed complete with the distribution of a registration number "and a [triangular piece of color-coded] cloth corresponding to the category to which he belonged."[5] The color for almost all priests was red, denoting their status as political prisoners.

One of the surviving records issued at Dachau documenting Fr. Johann (Jean) Bernard's arrival at Dachau and his prisoner number. Image courtesy of the United States Holocaust Memorial Museum

The registration process was now over, yet the humiliation was not. The prisoners were marched toward the quarantine block, also called "new-comer's barracks," where they would be held in isolation for a random duration. Ostensibly the seclusion was meant to prevent the spread of germs that the men might be incubating. In reality, it was a period of acclimation to the new life at Dachau. The brutal and uncertain length of seclusion caused profound anguish among the prisoners. "The priests in particular were confronted with difficulties because of their priesthood, which could earn them the hostility of some of [the communist] detainees,"[6] who often provoked verbal and physical abuses, all in an effort to scandalize a man of religion.

Fr. Bernard's entry into the quarantine barracks was quite eventful, albeit typical of life in Dachau. As he stepped over the threshold, the block senior struck him several times with his truncheon, an indication that he may have been moving too slowly. The "welcome to Dachau beating" caused the SS guard to burst out with laughter, which soon became a chorus as the other prisoners joined in. Laughter amongst the detainees was a rarity as the newcomers would soon learn. During their time in quarantine they would become acquainted with the new rules and procedures of camp life. Under the watchful eye of the block seniors, who acted as supervisors in charge of the units, and the SS officers who guarded them, the prisoners were assigned chores. The work was light and included cleaning and maintaining the barracks and restocking the supply room. Food was scarce and sleeping arrangements deplorable. Roll call, carried out three times a day, assembled in a narrow yard between barracks. It would last an endless amount of time and take place in any type of weather.

For Fr. Bernard, the son of a wealthy businessman from a luxurious background, who had been free to pray and serve God at any time and in any manner chosen by him, the first day at Dachau may have seemed harsh. He had no idea of the horrors that still awaited him.

Darkness at Dachau

PART I

Chapter 1

Germany in Decline
The First World War and Its Aftermath

World War I raged for four years beginning in 1914. During those years it involved most of the nations of Europe, as well as Russia, the United States, the Middle East and many other nations of the world. Billed as the war to end all wars, the conflict pitted the Central Powers of Germany, Austria-Hungary, and Turkey, against Great Britain, France, Italy, Japan, and eventually the United States, which joined the Allied effort in 1917.

It was the June 14, 1914 assassination of Archduke Franz Ferdinand, heir to the Austria-Hungarian Empire, and his wife, Sophie, that sparked the hostilities, but it was the imminent threat of invasion that prompted Germany to sign an armistice agreement with the Allied forces on November 11, 1918, marking the defeat of the Central Powers and the demoralization of Germany.

The war took an unprecedented toll in terms of slaughter, carnage, and destruction. Human casualties totaled nine-million dead and twenty-one million wounded. Germany alone accounted for about one million of those deaths. In addition to the combat casualties, disease, starvation or exposure combined to kill another five million civilians during the war years.

World War I caused economic and political disaster in much of the world, though it might be argued that no one suffered greater hardship than the people of Germany. In addition to the toll of human life, Germany suffered an extraordinary loss of property. As a result of signing the Treaty of Versailles, the victorious powers imposed punitive territorial, military, and

1

economic provisions on the defeated nation. In the west, Germany was forced to return to France Alsace-Lorraine, which it had seized more than forty years earlier. "Belgium received Eupen and Malmedy; the industrial Saar region was placed under the administration of the League of Nations for fifteen years; and Denmark received Northern Schleswig. Finally, the Rhineland was demilitarized; that is, no German military forces or fortifications were permitted there. In the east, Poland received parts of West Prussia and Silesia from Germany. In addition, Czechoslovakia obtained the Hultschin district from Germany; the largely German city of Danzig became a free city under the protection of the League of Nations; and Memel, a small strip of territory in East Prussia along the Baltic Sea, was ultimately placed under Lithuanian control. Outside Europe, Germany lost all its colonies. In sum, Germany forfeited 13 percent of its European territory (more than 27,000 square miles) and one-tenth of its population (between 6.5 and 7 million people)."[7]

Map showing the impact of the Treaty of Versailles on the German Nation. Source: The United States Holocaust Memorial Museum

The Treaty of Versailles even included a "'war guilt clause,' which identified Germany as the sole responsible party for the war and forced it to pay reparations," a debt that was calculated to take ninety-two years to repay. An ill-fated political response to meet that debt by printing more money further exacerbated Germany's problems and led to the collapse of its currency.

To fund the war, "Germany had suspended the gold standard and financed the war by borrowing. Reparations required under the treaty further strained the economic system, and the Weimar Republic printed more money as the mark's value tumbled." In 1920, hyperinflation rocked Germany, rendering 100,000 German marks comparatively valued at one American cent. By November 1923, it would require 42 billion marks to achieve the same value."[8] Wheelbarrows full of German marks would be required to purchase a few slices of bread.

The world tried to rescue Germany from the mountain of debt. "In 1924, the Dawes Plan reduced Germany's war debt and forced it to adopt a new currency. Reparations continued to be paid through a strange round robin: The U.S. lent Germany money to pay reparations, and the countries that collected reparations payments from Germany used that money to pay off United States debts."[9] The United States deemed the plan brilliant, and its success launched the career of Charles G. Dawes to new political heights when, in 1925, he was elected to serve as Vice President under President Calvin Coolidge. The world also thought the plan a novel approach and awarded Dawes a Nobel Prize for his role in the negotiation process that led to the implementation of it. Despite the envisioned success of the Dawes Plan, "the Weimar Republic still struggled to pay its debts, so another plan was hashed out in 1928. The Young Plan involved a reduction of Germany's war debt to just 121 billion gold marks."[10] Before this plan could take root, however, the stock market crashed on October 24, 1929, launching Germany into an economic Depression. Hundreds of people lost their jobs in a blink of the eye.

In 1931, U.S. President Herbert Hoover tried to help Germany avert disaster by placing a one-year moratorium on the German payment of reparations, and in 1932, "Allied delegates attempted to write off all Germany's reparations debt at the Lausanne Conference, but the U.S. Congress refused to sign on to the resolution. Germany was still on the hook for its war debt."[11]

The people of Germany suffered a perfect storm of humiliation. They were defeated militarily in the war and disgraced before the world when they were forced to sign the Treaty of Versailles. The noted British economist, John Maynard Keynes, said, "If we take the view that Germany must be kept impoverished and her children starved and crippled, vengeance, I dare say, will not limp."[12]

Keynes wasn't alone in his thinking. Many Americans were also hostile to the treaty and the U.S. Congress refused to ratify it. Senator Philander Chase Knox, who served in the cabinet of three presidents, said to U.S.President Woodrow Wilson, "I am convinced after the most painstaking consideration that I can give, that this treaty does not spell peace, but war. War more woeful and devastating than the one we have but now closed."[13]

Regardless of the objections, the treaty was signed, leading to perhaps the most devastating long-term impact on the once-proud people of Germany; the impression of utter and complete demoralization. As a result, "a whole generation of German children [grew] up humiliated and dreaming of revenge."[14]

Chapter 2

A "Savior" To Lead the German People

Out of the economic and political ashes resulting from fifteen years of decline arose a young dynamic leader who offered the promise of restored national pride, renewed dignity, economic stability, and a fresh solidarity based on the national exceptionalism of the German race.

Adolf Hitler was born in Braunau am Inn, Austria, on April 20, 1889 to Alois Hitler and Klara Poelzl. Described as a moody child, Adolf eventually grew hostile toward his father, an illegitimate child who had previously used his mother's maiden name of Schickelgruber. Alois died in 1903, however, shortly after moving his family to the outskirts of Linz, a move that young Adolf hated. The adolescent Hitler was exceptionally close to his mother, who happened to be overly lenient with him and didn't object to his dropping out of high school in 1905, at the age of sixteen, to become a painter.

In 1907, Hitler went to Vienna where he applied to the Viennese Academy of Fine Arts. With limited talent and no skill, Adolf's application for admission was twice rejected. Embittered, Hitler became increasingly angry. The death of his mother later that year further exacerbated his resentment, and understandably had a profound impact on the teenager. He returned to Vienna initially living with a successful friend, but later "moving from hostel to hostel as a lonely, vagabond figure."[15] Finally, settling in as a resident of a community "Men's Home," Hitler scraped out a living selling his art cheaply. He refused to admit failure even in the face of abject poverty.

At the same time, the young Hitler developed a world-view that centered on hatred for Jews and Marxists, attitudes "that would characterize his whole life."[16] It was at this time in Vienna that Hitler was noticeably influenced by the demagogy of Vienna's deeply anti-Semitic mayor Karl Lueger, "a man who used hate to help create a party of mass support. Adding to his hatred and hostility toward Jews and Catholics was Hitler's previous influence by Georg Ritter Von Schonerer, an Austrian politician openly opposed to liberals, socialists, Catholics, and Jews. The City of Vienna itself was highly anti-Semitic making Hitler's bigotry and hatred representative of the popular mindset. In that sense, his attitudes were not unusual and readily accepted as mainstream. What would prove to be profoundly unusual a decade or two later, however, was the extent to which Hitler would go to advocate these ideas to an audience that accepted them at unprecedented levels.

Hitler moved to Munich in 1913, but was found to be unfit for Austrian military service a year later when the assassination of Archduke Franz Ferdinand provided the spark that ignited World War I. Instead, Adolf joined the 16th Bavarian Infantry Regiment, serving as a corporal for the next four years after refusing a promotion. As a dispatch runner, he earned the Iron Cross on two occasions, was wounded twice and suffered a gas attack shortly before the end of the war, sending him to the hospital with temporary blindness. While recovering in the hospital, Hitler learned of Germany's surrender and considered the nation's action a betrayal.

Though despising the new socialist regime that now led the German nation, Hitler made a financial decision to remain in the military service until he could fulfill his own destiny of restoring Germany's military, economic, and social greatness. His anti-socialist sentiments attracted the attention of like-minded army officers "who were setting up anti-revolutionary units."[17]

In 1919, Hitler was assigned to spy on the German Worker's Party, a political party of about forty idealists dedicated to the belief in race science and the superiority of the Aryan race (or "German blood"). Rather than performing his ascribed duties, however, Hitler quickly realized that this group very closely reflected his own beliefs and he joined them. Using his skills as a public speaker, he quickly rose within the Party ranks and, by 1921, he was elected the group's chairman. He promptly renamed them the Socialist German Workers Party (NSDAP). He adopted the Swastika as a symbol and organized a personal army of "storm troopers" that he called the SA or Brownshirts. He also appointed bodyguards of black-shirted men for the purpose of attacking opponents. These men he called the *Schutzstaffel* or the SS.

Hitler's Party sustained substantial growth, and in November 1923, he organized Bavarian nationalists to a meeting in a beer hall in Munich to plan a coup, or '*putsch*,' and declare their new government. "Three thousand men marched through the streets, but they were met by police who opened fire, killing sixteen."[18]

In 1924, Hitler was arrested, but rather than dampening the Party's enthusiasm, Hitler "used his trial to spread his name and his ideas widely."[19] The five-year prison sentence he drew worked as a sign of implied accord with his views. He ended up serving only nine months of the sentence and used the solitude to write a book. *Mein Kampf* (My Struggle), a wildly successful volume that would sell some five-million copies over the next fifteen years, outlined the young leader's theories of Germany, race, and Jews.

It was also during, or shortly after, these nine months of incarceration that Hitler came to the narcissistic realization that he, and probably he alone, had the genius necessary to lead his nation. He resolved to accumulate as much power as he could through the subversion of the Weimar Republic, which had been in power since 1919. He methodically rebuilt the NSDAP into the Nazi Party and allied himself and his Party with people he determined would be relevant to the future. These included Hermann Goering, who would become a leader of the Nazi Party and one of the primary architects of the Nazi police state in Germany. Another Nazi Party notable was Joseph Goebbels, who became a very close confidant of Hitler's and was known for his lethal anti-Semitism and calls for the extermination of Jewish people. Goebbels was also a strong orator and a mastermind propagandist. Associates such as these created a treacherous atmosphere for Jews but proved a vital component of Hitler's quest for unmitigated power. With a team assembled, Hitler began to enhance his Nazi Party by both exploiting the fears of socialists and by appealing to anyone who believed their livelihood was threatened by the devastating economic depression of the 1930s.

Through a combination of his propaganda machine and the effectiveness of the public speaking of Party officials, the Nazis "gained the interest of big business, the press and the middle class,"[20] and were able to seat 107 members of the Reichstag in 1930. The Nazi Party that Hitler infiltrated was, in reality, comprised of a number of socialists, an ideology that Hitler despised. The Nazi Party that Hitler would mold, however, was based on race and not on the conceptual ideals of socialism.

Over the course of a few years, Hitler would complete the task of expelling all the socialists from the Party ranks, ensuring that the new Nazi Party could focus on the extermination of Jews and others who would impede his plan to create an Arian nation.

With his effective oration, Adolf Hitler also managed to capture the imagination of the disgraced German people, and in 1932, after becoming a German citizen, he ran for president. Though placing second to Paul Von Hindenburg, the Nazis added 123 more seats to the Reichstag, making them the largest Party in Germany. The new Party strength, coupled with factional differences that existed within the government, led to Hitler being appointed Chancellor of Germany on January 30, 1933, despite serving with a president who distrusted him. With relative speed, Hitler isolated and expelled his opponents from power, shutting trade unions and removing communists, conservatives, and Jews. When President Hindenburg died of heart failure on August 2, 1934, Hitler, who now had little opposition remaining in power, "integrated the Chancellorship and the Presidency, making him the sole Führer (or leader) of Germany."[21]

Hitler wasted no time taking the actions he deemed necessary to restore Germany to its former greatness. The accomplishment of this goal, he believed, required the simultaneous implementation of a two-pronged solution. Just two days after Hitler assumed the office of Chancellor, he addressed his nation by radio noting,

> "The misery of our people is horrible to behold! Along with the hungry unemployed millions of industrial workers there is the impoverishment of the whole middle class and the artisans. If this collapse finally also finishes off the German farmers, we will face a catastrophe of incalculable dimension. For that would be not just the collapse of a nation, but of a two-thousand-year-old inheritance of some of the greatest achievements of human culture and civilization..."[22]

He promised a new government that would "achieve the greatest task of reorganizing our nation's economy by means of two great four-year plans... Within four years, unemployment must be decisively overcome... The Marxist parties and their allies have had fourteen years to show what they can do. The result is a heap of ruins. Now, people of Germany, give us four years and then pass judgement upon us!"[23]

And Hitler delivered! First, he put the German people back to work in good-paying jobs. His economic policy, according to twentieth-century Canadian American economist John Kenneth Galbraith, was very different than the one employed in the United States by President Franklin Delano Roosevelt. The Hitler economic model involved "large scale borrowing for public expenditures, and at first this was principally for civilian work – railroads, canals and the "Autobahn" [highway network]. The result was a far more effective attack on unemployment than in any other industrial country."[24] As a result of the engagement of this approach, by late 1935, less than two years after Hitler's ascent to power, unemployment was at an end in Germany. "By 1936," Galbraith wrote, "high income was pulling up prices or making it possible to raise them."[25] To those who suffered from the losing war effort, a financial collapse and other economic strains, this was an achievement unparalleled.

Chapter 3

A Network of Concentration Camps and A Final Solution

> *"In Germany First they came for the communists*
> *And I did not speak out – because I was not a communist.*
> *Then they came for the Jews*
> *And I did not speak out – Because I was not a Jew.*
> *Then they came for the Catholics*
> *And I did not speak out – Because I was a Protestant.*
> *Then they came for me*
> *And there was no one left to speak out for me."*
> *-Pastor Martin Niemöller*

Nothing succeeds like success. It is no surprise, then, that a nation that had been oppressed and virtually paralyzed by economic fears, would respond so favorably to the new energetic leadership that Adolf Hitler offered. This newfound national popularism also enabled Hitler to enact the national-cleansing phase of his "make Germany Great Again" plan without reprisal. The execution of this phase required the construction of concentration camps that would ostensibly be used to detain enemies of state.

German concentration camps were nothing like modern-day prisons. They were outside of the country's legal system and therefore independent of any form of judicial review. There were, in fact, three primary reasons for the establishment of this Nazi network of camps: "To incarcerate real and perceived 'enemies of the state.' These persons were incarcerated for indefinite amounts of time; To eliminate individuals and small, targeted groups of individuals by murder, away from the public and judicial review; [and] To exploit forced labor of the prisoner population. This purpose grew out of a labor shortage."[26]

To achieve these goals, the Nazis established several types of camps. Not all of these sites were "concentration camps" under the strict definition, though they are often described that way in history. "Nazi-established sites included:

- **Concentration camps:** For the detention of civilians seen as real or perceived 'enemies of the Reich.'
- **Forced-labor camps:** In which the Nazi regime brutally exploited the labor of prisoners for economic gain and to meet labor shortages. Prisoners lacked proper equipment, clothing, nourishment, and rest.
- **Transit camps:** These functioned as temporary holding facilities for Jews awaiting deportation. These camps were usually the last stop before deportation to a killing center.
- **Prisoner-of-war camps:** For Allied prisoners of war, including Poles and Soviet soldiers.
- **Killing centers:** Established primarily or exclusively for the assembly-line style murder of large numbers of people immediately upon arrival to the site. There were 5 killing centers for the murder of primarily Jews. The term is also used to describe "euthanasia" sites for the murder of disabled patients."[27]

The first of the concentration camps was built at Dachau and opened in March of 1933, less than two months after Hitler became chancellor of Germany. Located just outside of Munich in the southern part of the country, the camp initially housed political prisoners. Those, in Hitler's view, who had oppressed his nation and posed a threat to his power. The "first group of detainees consisted primarily of socialists and communists."[28]

To run the camps, Hitler selected officials from his Nazi paramilitary organization, *"Schutzstaffel,"* more commonly known as the SS. Hilmar Wäckerle was chosen to serve as the first commandant of Dachau. From the very first day detainees were treated harshly, and on May 25, 1933, a thirty-three-year-old Munich schoolteacher by the name of Sebastian Nefzger, was beaten to death. While the SS claimed that Nefzger had committed suicide, an autopsy concluded that the cause of death was strangulation.

This photo of the main gate at the entrance to Dachau was taken by United States Liberators in 1945. (Photo credit: United States Holocaust Memorial Museum)

Wäckerle and his underlings at Dachau were indicted for murder by the Munich public prosecutor, but "the prosecutor was immediately overruled by Hitler, who issued an edict stating that Dachau and all other concentration camps were not subject to German law as it applied to German citizens. SS administrators alone would run the camps and hand out punishment as they saw fit."[29]

In June of 1933, Theodor Eicke replaced Wäckerle as commandant at the Dachau facility. He immediately set the tone for what life at camp under the new regime would be like by issuing regulations for the camp's daily operation. "Prisoners deemed guilty of rule breaking were to be brutally beaten. Those who plotted to escape, or espoused political views, were to be executed on the spot. Prisoners would not be allowed to defend themselves or protest this treatment. Eicke's regulations served as a blueprint for the operation of all concentration camps in Nazi Germany."[30]

Once a remedy was established for those who posed a threat to Hitler's political power, the Führer was free to turn his attention to his urgent matters of ethnic cleansing. He did this by passing a series of decrees known as the Nuremberg Laws. The first of these laws, passed on March 31, 1933, was a decree of the Berlin City Health Commissioner suspending Jewish doctors from the city's social welfare services. This was followed by a series of laws, implemented between April and October 1933 that removed Jews from government service; forbade Jews admission to the bar; limited the number of Jewish students in public schools; revoked the citizenship of naturalized Jews and "undesirables," and banned Jews from editorial posts. As these laws did not impact a great number of people, little attention was paid to them by the non-Jewish German population.

Over the course of the next six years, however, the Nuremberg Laws were expanded and became much more lethal. Jews were excluded from many professional positions including those of tax consultant, veterinarian, educator, auctioneer, gun merchant, and midwifery. In addition, Jews were prohibited from serving as an officer in the army; marrying or having sexual relations with persons of "German or German-related blood," changing their name; changing the name of a Jewish-owned business, and transferring assets from Jews to non-Jews in Germany.

Further, the laws that initially limited admittance of Jewish children to public schools now banned them outright; they closed all Jewish-owned businesses by excluding Jews from German economic life; cancelled all state contracts held with Jewish-owned firms; banned Jews from health spas; required Jews bearing names of "non-Jewish" origin to adopt an additional name of "Israel" for men and "Sara" for woman.

Finally, the Third Reich invalidated all German passports held by Jews until the old passports were surrendered and stamped with the letter "J." Freedom of movement was restricted for Jews. They were required to report all property in excess of 5,000 Reichsmarks, and they were prohibited from owning carrier pigeons or purchasing lottery tickets; Jews were required to turn in all their gold, silver, diamonds, and other valuables to the state without compensation.[31] None of these restrictions and requirements garnered much concern from the non-Jewish German people. In fact, many of them were convinced that Hitler's plan would indeed restore Germany to its former greatness.

By the late 1930s Hitler's economic and social cleansing agendas were merged. The concentration camps were expanded in number and, in 1938 the Führer's powerful ascent took a more violent and deadly turn. "On the evening of November 9 of that year, synagogues in Germany and Austria were burned and Jewish homes, schools and businesses were vandalized. Over thirty thousand Jews were arrested and dispatched to Dachau and the Buchenwald and Sachsenhausen concentration camps."[32] Almost half of those thirty thousand, approximately eleven-thousand Jewish detainees were imprisoned in Dachau.

In 1939 Hitler started to carry out plans of aggressive territorial expansion. His invasion of Poland effectively launched World War II in Europe. It was then that the prisoners at Dachau were relocated to the Buchenwald, Mauthausen and Flossenbuerg camps so that Dachau, at least temporarily, could be used as a training site for members of the newly established "Waffen-SS," an elite SS combat unit whose troops also helped run the concentration camps. By 1940, Dachau had been reconverted into a concentration camp."[33]

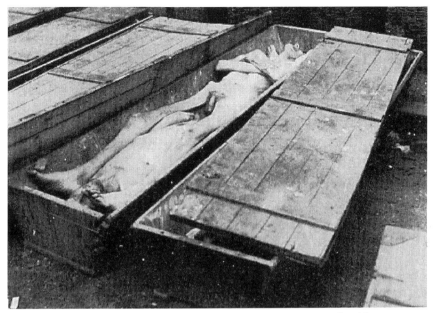

Allied forces photographed all corpses remaining at Dachau after liberation.
(Source: Report on the Liberation of Dachau.)

Conditions at the camp were both overcrowded and brutal. Designed to house approximately six thousand, the camp was satiated with thirty-thousand prisoners by 1944. The main camp was expanded to include a series of subcamps that were located around southern Germany and Austria. There, able-bodied prisoners were forced into slave labor to manufacture weapons and other materials needed by the German army to sustain the war effort.

About this same time, Hitler realized that his original plan of restricting Jewish activity throughout Germany and its annexed countries would not resolve his "Jewish problem." His isolated acts of violence, he reasoned, were equally ineffective. The only way Hitler could achieve his objective of creating a pure Aryan race would be the elimination of every European Jew and any other group considered by him to be unsuitable to reside in the new Germany. These deplorables, Hitler reasoned, "included artists; intellectuals and other independent thinkers; communists; Jehovah's Witnesses and others who were ideologically opposed to the

Nazi Party; homosexuals and others viewed as sexually deviant; Gypsies; the physically and mentally handicapped; and anyone else considered to be racially or physically impure."[34]

Between 1941 and 1944, Dachau's satellite camps exterminated thousands of prisoners considered sick or handicapped. Dachau was also "home" to several thousand members of the Catholic clergy. Father Titus Brandsma was one such clergyman. A Carmelite cleric, philosopher, writer, teacher, and historian, Brandsma was an avowed anti-Nazi. One month after his arrival at Dachau, he was euthanized by lethal injection. Father Michal Kozal was a Polish priest who arrived in Dachau in 1941. He attended to the spiritual needs of his fellow prisoners for about two years before being killed in the same fashion. Both men were beatified by Pope John Paul II in 1985 and 1987, respectively, and await sainthood in the Catholic Church.

Dachau was considered one of the most brutal labor camps in the network of Nazi concentration camps. Thousands of prisoners perished from disease, malnutrition, and overwork. Thousands more were brutally beaten for an infraction of camp rules and died as a result. Others were simply executed for challenging the rules. A group of Russians sent to Dachau in 1941 were summarily executed at a nearby rifle range. In 1942, with the full-throttled implementation of Hitler's final solution well underway, four sizeable ovens were built on site to incinerate the corpses of those murdered there. These proved inadequate, however, and "many Dachau detainees were moved to Nazi extermination camps in Poland, where they died in gas chambers."[35]

Dachau prisoners were also used as subjects in brutal Nazi experiments. In one such experiment prisoners were immersed in tanks of water chilled with ice for hours at a time to determine the feasibility of reviving them. Many prisoners died during their submersions.

From its opening in March of 1933 until the liberation of prisoners by United States forces on April 29, 1945, more than two-hundred-thousand prisoners were cataloged as having passed through the gates of Dachau. Thousands of others were never registered, making it virtually impossible to determine exactly how many people were imprisoned or died there.

While the Nazi Party managed to establish financial stability through a mixed economy, it became increasingly obvious, through the decade of the 1930s, that Hitler's goal was absolute dictatorship. All opposition was violently suppressed, and severe censorship was the order. Even artistic expression was being controlled. Moreover, when the racial order was instituted, Jews began to be slowly discriminated against and stigmatized. School syllabi were altered to preach racial biology to indoctrinate the young and instill hatred and prejudice deeply within their minds. Consequently, after a few years of relentless brainwashing, any trace of objection by anyone of influence to the horrors being perpetrated on the Jews and the others who were rounded up and removed from society was virtually nonexistent. Very few people outside of the SS who operated the death camps even knew of the intense brutality taking place within the confines of the camp walls, and few bothered to explore it. It's impossible to know how many really would have cared anyway.

Part II

Chapter 4

Concentration Camps Established
Throughout Occupied Europe

In addition to the camp at Dachau, an entire network of concentration camps was established throughout Germany and the territories it acquired. Some of these were opened shortly after completion of the camp at Dachau. Others were constructed later as the German territory expanded and demand rose.

To satisfy Hitler's insatiable lust for power and total domination, Nazi Germany expanded its boundaries through conquest. At first these invasions were relatively bloodless such as the conquests of Austria and Czechoslovakia in 1938 and 1939. The addition of new territory, however, quickly required the establishment of new camps in which to house the inflated number of the undesirables in German society. "By the time the Germans invaded Poland in September 1939, unleashing World War II, there were six concentration camps in the so-called Greater German Reich: **Dachau** (founded 1933), **Sachsenhausen** (1936), **Buchenwald** (1937), **Flossenburg**, in northeastern Bavaria near the Czech border (1938), **Mauthausen**, near Linz, Austria (1938), and **Ravensbrück**, the women's camp, established in Brandenburg Province, southeast of Berlin (1939), after the dissolution of Lichtenburg."[36]

Within a year of the invasion of Poland, the vast increase in camp inhabitants required a massive expansion of concentration camps to the east. "The climate of national emergency that the conflict granted to the Nazi leaders [also] permitted the SS to expand the functions of the camps."[37] Now, the SS saw the camps as opportunity zones, enabling them

21

to destroy enemies of Nazi Germany, whether real or perceived, without fear of reprisal. Within these zones, SS authorities could torture, starve, overwork, beat, and kill anyone they considered subhuman or a threat to the Third Reich. The camps became holding centers for a pool of slave labor that could be used for Nazi construction projects as well as for the production of armaments, weapons, and other goods that were needed for the German war effort. In addition, the prisoners were used by the SS as punching bags to release tension through unwarranted and unprovoked beatings; as lab rats to perform medical and non-medical experimentation; and as subservient vessels that could be used for the general entertainment of the SS.

Concentration Camps in operation in 1933 and 1934. By 1945, the Nazis constructed and filled over 1,000 camps and satellite camps in and around Germany. (Source: The United States Holocaust Memorial Museum)

By 1940, there were so many Polish prisoners, mostly people of Catholic faith, held within the confines of the camps that the Nazis were forced to construct six additional camps in Poland. These included **Chelmno, Treblinka, Sobibor, Majdanek, Belzec,** and the infamous **Auschwitz.** All of these became killing camps. In addition, there were subcamps built around the major camp facilities. These included **Wiener**

Neudorf, a subcamp of Mauthausen (1943), **Sosnowitz**, the subcamp of **Auschwitz III/Monowitz**, and hundreds of others.

Within the pre-expansion borders of Germany, the Nazis also constructed additional camps. These included **Kislav**, **Sachsenburg**, **Chemnitz**, **Coditz**, **Litchenburg**, **Breitenau**, **Kemna**, **Columbia Haus**, **Oranienburg**, **Missler**, **Esterwegen**, **Eutin**, and twenty-seven others.

In all, the Germans had more than one-thousand camps. Some of them were holding camps, some were killing camps, and some were labor camps, but all abused the detainees by exposing them to some of the most horrific brutalities that one man can exact on another.

Chapter 5

Masters of Torture

From May 1933 at least until the Nazi camps were liberated by Allied forces in April 1945, the German SS seemed to have perfected the art of both mental and physical torture. This was done systematically by quickly stripping a once proud and confident inmate of his dignity and then by slowly and painfully wiping away all remnants of physical and emotional strength until the release of death was preferable to another day of painful and laborious living.

Those newly arrested, or those previously rounded up and sent to one of the many ghettos, were given just minutes to pack one suitcase. The dehumanization process began as soon as the prisoner was marshaled for transportation to one of the camps. The preferred method of moving detainees was by railway, but not in luxurious passenger trains or even stuffy rail cars. Rather, those unfortunate enough to be a Jew, a Pole, a Gypsy, a dissident, a communist, a socialist, or any other person deemed unworthy by the Nazi Party, were transported via cattle and freight cars on the Deutsche Reichsbahn, a national railway system controlled by the Nazi Party and its allies for the sole purpose of the deportation of Jews and other victims of the Holocaust to one of the several Nazi camps.

Rather than the expected fifty people per car that conformed to the SS regulations, the Nazis forced one-hundred-and-fifty people to cram into a single car. These rail cars were packed so densely that the prisoners were forced to stand shoulder to shoulder for the entire trip. To make matters worse, the trains were given a low priority and proceeded to the mainline only after all other transports and military trains were allowed through.

This inevitably caused delays to the expected arrival time. While the average transport took about four days, the longest-known transport took eighteen days. When that train arrived at the camp from Corfu, everyone on board was already dead. "At times, the Germans did not have enough filled cars ready to start a major shipment of Jews to the camps, so victims were kept locked inside overnight at layover yards."[38]

Dachau prisoners march in formation carrying their bowls.
(Photo credit: United States Holocaust Memorial Museum)

During the time of transport, the detainees were denied food and water. There were no bathroom facilities, but rather only a single bucket in each car, forcing most to relieve themselves in their clothes, unable to even move away from the stench of those standing right next to them.

The extreme seasonal temperature variations were also a significant survival factor during transport. The summer temperature rose significantly in the windowless freight cars. Coupled with body heat generated in the crammed cars, many died of asphyxiation or heat stroke. In the winter months, those traveling in the cattle car, with its open, barred window high on the wall, caused many to die from exposure. Typically, a great many detainees perished long before their arrival at the designated camp. The survivors were forced to continue their travel with the corpses and the stench of rotting flesh and bodily excrement.

Frightened and confused family members clung to each other for as long as possible until the train arrived at the camp. When the doors were opened, the crushing push from behind caused some of those closest to the doors to fall approximately four feet to the ground. Others carefully lowered themselves while still others slid to the ground, too weak to jump from the train. Once on the terrain they were assisted by others who held them up in an effort to prevent them from being sent to the gas chambers, rifle range or hanging trees because of their infirmity or weakened condition.

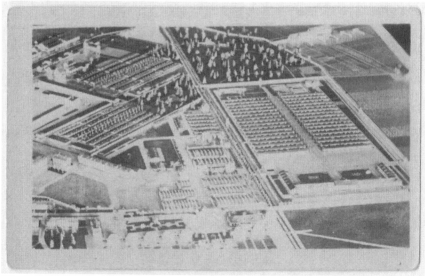

Photo of postwar model of Dachau (Photo Credit: United States Holocaust Memorial Museum, Norman Coulson Collection.

Men were immediately separated from women and children. People possessing a special skill were asked to identify themselves. Those fortunate enough to have worked as a tailor, a goldsmith, a cobbler, or in some other useful profession in their prior employment were removed from the line and designated for special assignment. These were the lucky ones slated for a work assignment in a service building where they would be required to utilize their skills in service of the SS officers. Because of the officers' need for their services, their treatment, while still abhorrent, was a cut above that of the average inmate. Jewish doctors were forced to work as camp physicians while the SS had no particular use, but rather intense disdain, for those whose profession had been the law. While the prisoners were being segregated, their hastily packed suitcases were tossed in rows for collection.

Weak, hungry, thirsty, and exhausted, the segregated detainees were forced to march, suitcase in hand, to the appropriate barrack. The Dachau facility was the largest camp in Germany consisting of one square mile, so it was no leisurely jaunt for someone who had been standing with no food or water for so long. The entire facility was enclosed by a seven-foot-high concrete wall that was covered with barbed wire. The prisoners were directed to the southwest corner of the camp where thirteen crude barracks stood. Originally built for military purposes, the barracks were in exceptionally poor condition due to sixteen years of weathering followed by only a superficial restoration when they served as a shelter for some eighteen-hundred Bavarian workmen who were deemed political adversaries of the Reich. (The number of barracks was later increased to thirty-four following the expansion of 1937 and 38.) The entire southwest quadrant was enclosed "by a high wire entanglement. The prisoners were warned that these were live wires,"[39] but that often proved to be untrue.

The initial number of detainees at Dachau totaled about seventeen hundred. The majority of these were Communists or members of Communist sympathizer groups such as the Workers' Athletic and Relief Organizations. About one-hundred prisoners were

> "Social Democrats, Socialist Workers Party members, students, lawyers and doctors, who were either active politically or known as pacifists. There were about forty Jews, mostly manual workers or clerks. A few of them were businessmen from small villages in northern Bavaria who had been arrested [because of] motives of personal rancor or envy. None of the prisoners could [have been] convicted of any violation of law, but they [were] nevertheless detained for an indefinite period."[40]

27

According to a Report published in *The New Republic* on August 8, 1934, which was deemed reliable and credible despite the anonymity of the author for safety reasons, each barrack was approximately one hundred meters (three-hundred-twenty-eight feet) long by ten meters (thirty-two feet) wide and comprised of five connecting rooms each lodging fifty-two prisoners. The rooms were equipped with rows of connecting three-level bunk beds, rough tables and benches all sitting on a concrete floor. Extraordinarily thin walls and poorly fitted windows failed to protect the prisoners from severe drafts of cold air, penetrating rain or wind. One small washstand was provided for all fifty-two occupants, who had to complete the task of washing in only twenty-five minutes, the equivalent of forty-eight seconds per man.

The bunks were layered three high, and all were attached as if they were one large row of singular construction. They were composed of wooden planks and topped with a round straw sack. Regardless, the SS required that the bed be made with four neat corners topped with a sheet positioned with sharp corners. The task of making a bed appear neat was near impossible to achieve, yet prisoners were forced to do so in little time lest they subject themselves to brutal beatings by the capo or SS Guards.

Fr. Jean Bernard, a Catholic priest imprisoned in Dachau in May 1941 for denouncing Nazis' from the pulpit, described the tedious and mind-numbing process. "Make the beds! Oh, what a dreadful order, mirroring the whole bloody stupidity of camp discipline. A straw sack is naturally round. But it has to have corners! Like a cigar box. […] Planks and little boards surface out of hiding places, specially carved for this purpose. Through a slit in the sack the straw is bulked up with a stick and stuffed against the edge, then a little board is held against it to press it flat. The sheet is carefully spanned over it and a sharp edge is ironed in on the side."[41]

Each barrack was designed to house between one-hundred-and-fifty to two-hundred people, but by the end of the war, as many as two-thousand prisoners were packed into the space. Some of the barracks were used to house the canteen, the camp orderly room, the sickbay and the punishment blocks. There was also a quarantine barracks for those just arriving.[42]

The Dachau bunks just after the camp's liberation by United States forces in May 1945. Although the original design of each bunk was for one person, overcrowding at the camp in the latter war years required that up to six people share a single bunk. (Photo credit: United States Holocaust Memorial Museum)

As the men and women made their way into their respective barracks, they could not conceive of the horrors that awaited them. They would find out in very short order. Male prisoners were forced to work at "hard labor, building roads and laying out drilling and shooting grounds."[43] To accomplish this work, prisoners were harnessed to a heavy roller, which they were forced to pull for nine hours each and every day while others, who were constructing a swimming pool for the guards, were required to stand in cold water excavating quicksand to make a hole for the pool's foundation. The men grew weary, but if work slowed, they were kicked or lashed by the guards causing some to collapse.

For a few short days the camp was commanded by the regular police force. They were soon replaced, however, by the Nazi SS, and that's when the intimidating language began. As was probably intended, prisoners could easily overhear the camp leader's speech to his subordinates: "Always remember that no human beings are here, only swine. Whoever does not wish to see blood may go home immediately. No one who does harm to a prisoner need fear reprimand. The more you shoot, the fewer we must feed."[44] Some of the inmates may have thought

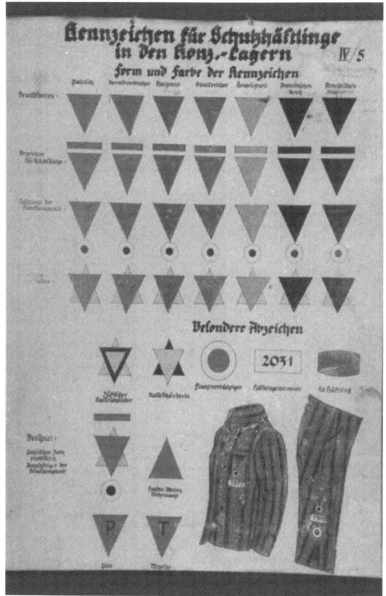

The chart above shows the prisoner markings used in German concentration camps including the Dachau Camp in Germany, ca. 1938-1942.
Beginning in 1937–1938, the SS created a system of marking prisoners in concentration camps. Sewn onto uniforms, the color-coded badges identified the reason for an individual's incarceration, with some variation among camps. The Nazis used this chart illustrating prisoner markings in the Dachau concentration camp.[45] (Image courtesy of the United States Holocaust Memorial Museum.)

that these words were nothing more than scare tactics. They found out all too soon exactly how true those words were.

In Dachau, and eventually in all camps, certain prisoners were selected and forced to work as capos, meaning that they had to preside over the activities of the barrack. They were required to ensure that all men of that barrack followed the rules of the camp, demanding that the prisoners were on time for muster, that they didn't take too much time for meals or breaks, that they kept the barrack neat and clean, their beds appropriately made, etc. They forced compliance by beating the other prisoners, and if the beating wasn't severe enough to keep the prisoners in line, then the capo himself was beaten by the SS officers. The beatings that the capo inflicted increased in intensity each time such discipline was imposed. This was due in part to the capo's desire to avoid personal beatings by the SS and in part to demonstrate to the SS his own brutality toward his fellow inmates, thereby assuring his continued role as capo. Pitting inmate against inmate was one more way for the SS to inflict psychological torture on the prisoners in an effort to break their spirits.

To further accentuate the dehumanization process, identification numbers were assigned to the inmates, and from that moment, they were referred to, not by name, but by number. Josef Felder, a legislator who voted against the 1933 law that entrenched the Nazi power, and who was imprisoned at Dachau from 1935 to 1936 as a result, recalled that inmates "were stripped of their clothes, names and all human dignity. They were given a number and a category. They were handed a cloth to wear according to their category. This [the category assigned] was often the difference between life and death."[46]

Prisoners had to appear two times a day, every day of the year, in all weather, on a grassy square in front of the administration building. "If a prisoner was missing from roll call, usually due to illness, then the others often had to stand on the spot for hours on end."[47] Sometimes these musters would last for many hours and the men were forced to stand at attention until told otherwise. In the winter months, some simply froze to death. In the summer, it was heat exhaustion that would take their lives.

Josef Joos was a member of Parliament. As such, he was one of the most vocal supporters of the Christian Democratic Union in Germany.

He was arrested for his convictions and spent almost four years, from 1941 to 1945, as a prisoner at Dachau. He described everyday life at the camp:

> "Always awake. You can never forget where you are. You had to be on your guard at all times. If there was a bad mood on.[the] part of the camp leader or block senior and you came under their spotlight, you were humiliated, trodden on, sworn at and beaten. As a punishment we had to stand on the campground for hours on end through all weathers, being deprived of food and beaten with sticks. It was a depressing feeling to have no rights and no protection against the oppressor."[48]

Dachau prisoners immediately following liberation. (Source: Report on the Liberation of Dachau.)

All clothes were relinquished, and the inmates were ordered to take striped "pajamas" woven from a very course fiber, a matching striped hat, and wooden clogs from a mountain of clothes that lay there. Nothing was sized properly, and prisoners weren't allowed time to look for something that actually fit or even fit better. They were forced to simply take the next article of clothing on the pile. Many prisoners found it was near impossible to keep the wooden clogs on their feet without painfully curling the toes making each step excruciating.

Felder explained his experience this way:

"When we arrived at camp, we had our heads shaved and then we were given course prison clothes to wear. Then we were marched to the commandant's office. With a leather whip we were given twenty-five lashes on our naked behinds. This was in accordance with the camp rules. They often deliberately miscounted strokes and started all over again. Most of the time they decided themselves the number of strokes they applied and made sure they exceeded the limit. With no attention to our flesh wounds, we were ordered to dress and then we were thrown out into the yard."[49]

By this time, all individualism was lost as each prisoner looked and felt like the next.

Prisoners were briefly informed of the extensive camp rules. Very often, the rules were too much for a prisoner to remember especially in their worn-down condition at the time the rules were explained. Regardless, any violations of those rules were punished in the most severe way. Often, a prisoner who did not make up his bed properly, took too long to eat, or broke one of the hundreds of other rules, was hung on a poll. With his hands tied behind his back, the prisoner was hoisted up the poll by a rope tied at the wrist. The weight of the body was enough to immediately dislocate the arms from their shoulder sockets. Sometimes a prisoner was left hanging this way for days.

"A favorite stunt of the Nazis [was] to order newly arrived prisoners into a dark room and make them stand with their faces against the wall while volleys [of gun shots were] fired into the air. Whenever a new transport [arrived], some prisoners [were] picked out and horribly beaten with wired oxtails."[50] On April 12, a transport from Nuremberg arrived with three Jewish prisoners. The story of these three, and a fourth Jew by the name of Erwin Kahn, who had been imprisoned at least since March 1933, was about to become legendary throughout the camp.

A successful businessman from Munich, Kahn's life was irreparably altered early in 1933. As he strolled down the street, Kahn was approached by an SS man and taken into protective custody at the Stadelheim prison. He was charged with being a member of the German Communist Party (KPD). He was sure that the officer was mistaken and was confident that the misunderstanding would be cleared up on relatively short order.

Rather than being released, however, Kahn was transferred to Dachau concentration camp, becoming one of its first prisoners.

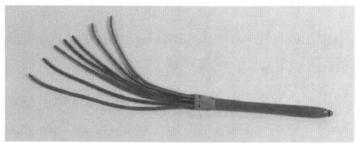

Whip used to administer beatings - This one was taken from a Dachau Guard by William Weinberg, Company B, 15th Infantry Regiment of the 3rd Division (Photo credit: United States Holocaust Memorial Museum)

Whipping block from Dachau. Prisoners would be forced to drop their trousers, kneel on the wooden side-kneeler and bend over the length of the block. Guards would then use a leather whip to beat their naked buttocks. (Photo credit: United States Holocaust Memorial Museum.)

Photo displayed at the Dachau Concentration Camp Memorial Site in Germany showing prisoners hanging by the arms on poles. With arms tied behind their backs, prisoners' shoulders would be dislocated almost immediately upon being hoisted.

While cause for concern, this did not dampen Kahn's optimistic spirit. On March 23, he wrote a letter to his wife, Evi, providing assurances that she need not be overly concerned. He did not belong to the German Communist Party and was certain that, once interviewed by the prison sentries, the matter would be cleared up rather quickly. He noted that the treatment at the camp had been "very good," as was the food. He described his cellmates as "very pleasant...mostly good sorts." He concluded the letter by asking Evi to send cigarettes, matches, a newspaper and "some thick socks as the floor of his cell was cold."[51]

The following week, Kahn wrote to Evi again, but mentioned nothing of a release. Still upbeat, he told her of a six-hour-per-day work assignment for which he was grateful. Able to receive inspected packages, Kahn asked his wife to send toothpaste, butter, marmalade, meat paste, plums, cake, hard-boiled eggs, and his pipe now that the smoking ban was to be lifted.

A third letter dated April 5, shows that Kahn "remained guardedly optimistic that everything would be resolved as soon as the police got 'round to interrogating him." Evi's letters were a consolation amidst uncertainty and 'on the whole,' he concluded, 'I can't really complain.'"[52]

That all changed on the evening of April 12 when Kahn, and the three other Jewish prisoners who had just arrived were taken out to the woods on the mendacious grounds and shot, ostensibly while trying to escape. The other three men died instantly, but Kahn, despite being shot five times a point-blank range, survived and was taken to the Schwabing hospital. He lived for five days, and though in critical condition, he was able to make a statement to his fellow prisoners assuring them that no attempt to escape had been made.

Nevertheless, the next morning the prisoners were addressed by one of the SS guards. He began by insulting the Jews: "They successfully tried to mislead and to stir up hatred and strife among the German people. But when they have to share your lot and wield pick and shovel as you do, they try to escape." Three of the four prisoners were shot by Second-in-Command Erpsmüller, who boasted about the deed before the prisoners and remarked, "I am opposed to torture for the Jews. Bugs are not exterminated by tearing out their legs but are trampled upon."[53] Kahn became the twelfth prisoner executed at Dachau in just two months. He may well have been a victim of mistaken identity as he had assumed, but he was, nevertheless, a Bavarian Jew. That alone could have warranted a death sentence in Nazi Germany.

Despite the intensity of the labor, the men were fed only three pounds of bread every three days. Each day they would be given two bowls of coffee, one in the morning and another in the evening. The daily lunch consisted of a small plate that was seventy-five-percent potatoes and twenty-five-percent meat or vegetable. This was an insufficient amount of food for someone working so hard for so long. Consequently, it was not uncommon for men to lose up to one-hundred pounds over the span of just a few months.

The quality of sleep was about as inadequate as the daily nutrition plan. Frequently, intoxicated SS guards ran through the room waving their guns, ripping prisoners out of their beds and inflicting beatings that left some requiring medical attention. The strain alone caused the inmates' hair to turn white.

For Joseph Goetz, imprisoned because of his affiliation with the Communist Party, for which he served as secretary, the late nights were particularly painful. Initially, he was frequently taken from his cell for cross-examination only to return covered with wounds. The barrack orderly refused to treat him. Later, SS guards would skip the ruse of interrogation altogether. Rather, each

"night at 10 o'clock, Steinbrenner, one of the overseers entered the cell with five other special policemen equipped with long oxtails. They beat him into unconsciousness. The mattress, drenched with blood, was put out to dry in the sun every second day. After having gone through this torture for more than two weeks, Goetz was killed in his cell. His coffin was made in the cabinet-makers' workshop by his former friends. In the meantime, his corpse lay in a coal cellar, the bleeding head wrapped in newspapers."[54]

Goetz wasn't the only person to suffer such cruelties at the hands of Dachau's SS officers. Deputy Fritz Dressel, too, was subjected to daily torture until he tried to cut his wrist with a piece of glass. He was discovered while still showing signs of life and was taken to a first-aid station where his wound was dressed. Immediately thereafter, he was ordered back to his detention cell by Camp Commander Hilmar Wäckerle, against the doctor's advice. Dressel was discovered a few hours later in his cell with the dressing ripped off, lying in a pool of blood. Both arms had been pulled from their sockets.

On another day, a transport arrived with two-hundred men from the northern region of Bavaria. It was obvious that some of them had been badly beaten either before or during transport. Upon arrival, twelve Jews were selected from those transported and taken to the guard room.

"They were stripped of their clothing; their heads were wrapped in blankets to smother their cries and they were beaten barbarously. Later, after kicks on the testicles and further beatings, they were driven to the barracks. The body of each, from the waist to the knee, was one complete wound. The entire scene took place in the presence of a high official, Dr. Frank, and fifteen Special

Police headed by Steinbrenner, Hofmann and Kantschuster."[55]

One of the twelve beaten men died of his injuries shortly thereafter. Normally, the cause of death in such cases was listed as "Shot while trying to escape," or "Found hanged in his cell." In this case, though, neither cause of death would suffice because there was no gunshot wound or neck abrasions. The dilemma posed no problem for the SS because that same night the shed in which the body was laid out was torched, destroying the body and all evidence of the beating. The official announcement listed the cause of death as heart disease, and the body was returned to the parents in a sealed coffin.

Major Hungbinger was a member of the Nazi party but was accused of being a spy. He too was "tortured in his cell and hanged himself with a rope that is always provided for this purpose in the detention cells. As soon as the noose was taken off the body, Overseer Vogel laughingly showed the bloodstained rope to the other prisoners."[56]

Commander Erpsmüller personally supervised some of the tortures as was the case with the beating of Mr. Schloss, a businessman from Nuremberg. He was struck repeatedly on the testicles for three days before succumbing to his injuries. "Jews were forced to scrub especially befouled toilets with their bare hands"[57] and, at times, made to smear the excrement on their faces. Two prisoners were taken to a nearby brook into which entangled barbed wire had been discarded. Made to work without shoes or gloves, the men were forced to remove the barbed wire until the brook was clean. They returned to the camp "benumbed with cold and with their hands and feet severely lacerated."[58]

Survivors of the abusive beatings were no better off than their counterparts who died as a result. They were treated by camp "doctors." These "doctors," however, had no medical training. They were male German prisoners who were given no instruction whatsoever. They were simply assigned the task of looking after patients. Stanislav Kamechik, a Czech prisoner who was forced to work in the infirmary, wrote in a statement that the prisoners assigned this task included

"quite a few criminal elements which could dispose of the life and death of their patients as they pleased. There was no control at all. In the surgical department all the material available was one pair of scissors, a pair of pincers (forceps), and a few liniments and paper bandages."[59]

Many prisoners were afflicted with diarrhea, something especially frowned upon by the guards. As punishment, such patients were tied down to a special bed. "This bed stood under a cold shower which was turned on during the whole night...It is unnecessary to say that the treatment was a fatal one."[60]

Barracks 1 and 7 had a different way of treating such patients. There, "a bed was placed in the lavatory for the dying, the very serious cases, or those who had dirtied their beds. Very often patients were put there because they had gold teeth or money which, at that time, was still allowed in the camp. Out of this bed no patient ever escaped alive. If he did not die quickly enough, the Chief of the Barracks (*Oberpfleger*) who was a German by the name of Max Kolb (an anti-social element with a black triangle) gave him an intravenous injection of gasoline."[61]

According to Kamechik, prisoners assigned to the infirmary were also required to assist in the performance of surgeries on other prisoners. Here, the medical ignorance was on full display. Aqua distillate, a strong clear Scandinavian liquor distilled from potato or grain mash and flavored with caraway seed, was used as a disinfectant. On one particular patient, Kolb made an incision using a scalpel he had taken from the room where the dead were sectioned. There was no clear objective to the surgery, he simply made an incision on every part of the man that looked swollen. Surgeons operated whenever they wanted regardless of the medical necessity of the surgery. "For example, they simply said, 'Tomorrow I want to make a stomach resection and I want to operate [on] two [people with an] appendix [problem],' and they were made accordingly."[62]

The chief capo, Josef Hayden, also performed surgeries on prisoners. Described as a scoundrel and a sadist who beat a few prisoners to death every day, Hayden started his surgical career by amputating fingers without anesthesia. According to Kamechik, "...the department for surgical cases was full of patients with their finger or fingers cut because everyone that came into the ambulance with a little wound on his finger was sure to lose it." The finger amputations satisfied Hayden's lust for blood and the infliction of pain for a couple of months "then he began with hand amputations. Fortunately, this period did not last very long as he felt himself more attracted by appendectomy operations."[63] Hayden was about to advance to stomach and brain surgery when he was released and came to the SS probably because they "recognized him as a member of their honor society."[64]

Hayden was replaced by Karl Zimmerman, who had been in charge of the infectious disease section. Immediately he used his expertise to separate the serious cases, sending them to his former unit. "There went a rumor that they were all killed by infections."[65]

In 1942 the first real doctors were sent to the Dachau infirmary to make preparations in the pathological anatomy department. There were already two prisoners in this department who specialized in preparing human skin for lamp shades or book covers if the skin contained tattoos. For Christmas the following year Dr. Karr, one of the new physicians, ordered a present for his wife; "a pair of slippers made from human skin."[66]

The Nazis even conditioned and utilized dogs to facilitate the torture of prisoners. Dachau kept about fifty to sixty dogs for this purpose. SS Guard Paul Henss was one of the Dachau dog handlers. His job was to train dogs to "bite without mercy and to literally tear prisoners to pieces if they attempted escape."[67] As part of the training, dogs were routinely starved in order to increase the ferocity of their attacks. Once unleashed on a prisoner, the dog would attack so viciously that even beating it with a club, as some prisoners did, would not deter a ravenous dog from its mission.

According to details described in a 1945 letter written by then twenty-nine-year-old Leon Morin to his family, two dogs got into a fight over a prisoner's half-eaten detached foot that was exhumed by them from a bone pit. One of the dogs managed to run through a fence and into a nearby town with the foot in his mouth.

At Dachau, there was no end to the torture. One man, who had been badly beaten, was lying on the concrete floor of the barrack when Commander Wäckerle entered. Upset that the man did not rise to attention, Wäckerle had the man removed and his wounds dressed so that he would be conscious when the beating resumed.

Mr. Strauss, an attorney from Munich, arrived at camp in good health. On relative short order, he was "transformed into a quivering white-haired old man. They compelled him to swim in ice-cold water while they lashed him with oxtails. After four days of torture he was shot."[68]

Morin's mention of Strauss swimming in ice-cold water may well be a reference to the medical experiments that were performed at Dachau by doctors of the SS under the direction of Captain Rash of the Luftwaffe, the aerial warfare branch of the German military. These experiments took place in the early 1940s at Dachau and were equally barbaric in their methods as the other prisoner tortures that occurred routinely. During the air warfare experiments young, healthy boys were placed into a chamber in which oxygen was slowly removed, simulating the natural oxygen levels available at various altitudes. Boys were deprived of oxygen until they passed into unconsciousness. Attempts were then made at revival, but it was too late for many who died from the lack of oxygen to the brain.

In a letter written by Dr. Sigmund Rascher to Heinrich Himmler on May 15, 1941, Rascher requested permission to conduct research on the effect of high altitudes upon pilots using inmates at the concentration camps. He received the following reply from SS Sturmbannfuehrer Karl Brandt, Himmler's adjutant, on May 22, 1941:

"Shortly before flying to Oslo, the Reichsfuehrer SS gave me your letter of 15 May 1941 for partial reply. I can inform you that prisoners will, of course, be made available gladly for the high-flight research. I have informed the Chief of the Security Police of this agreement of the Reichsfuehrer SS and requested that the competent official be instructed to get in touch with you."[69]

The subsequent experimentation was horrifying. Anton Pacholegg, an assistant to Dr. Rascher and an affiant at the Nuremberg war-crime trials of 1945-46, provided an eye-witness account of the low-pressure experiments conducted at Dachau:

Paul F. Caranci

This photo demonstrates how prisoners were positioned in a high-altitude compression chamber during experimentation. (Photo credit: United States Holocaust Memorial Museum)

"I have personally seen, through the observation window of the chamber, when a prisoner inside would stand a vacuum until his lungs ruptured. Some experiments gave men such pressure in their heads that they would go mad and pull out their hair in an effort to relieve the pressure. They would tear their heads and faces with their fingers and nails in an attempt to maim themselves in their madness. They would beat the walls with their hands and head and scream in an effort to relieve pressure on their eardrums. These cases of extremes of vacuums generally ended in the death of the subject. An extreme experiment was so certain to result in death that in many instances the chamber was used for routine execution purposes rather than as an experiment."[70]

Another trial witness, Franz Blaha from Czechoslovakia, who was held prisoner at Dachau from April 1941 until April 1945, testified:

"In 1942 and 1943 experiments on human beings were conducted by Dr. Sigmund Rascher to determine the effects of changing air pressure. As many as 25 persons were put at one time into a specially constructed van in which pressure could be increased or decreased as required. The purpose was to find out the effects on human beings of high altitude and of rapid descents by parachute. Through a window in the van I have seen the people lying on the floor of the van. Most of the prisoners used died from these experiments, from internal hemorrhage of the lungs or brain. The survivors coughed blood when taken out. It was my job to take the bodies out and as soon as they were found to be dead to send the internal organs to Munich for study. About 400 to 500 prisoners were experimented on. The survivors were sent to invalid blocks and liquidated shortly afterward. Only a few escaped."[71]

Later, in an effort to determine the survival potential of airmen downed at sea, a basin was constructed measuring 2.5 meters (8.2 feet) x 2.5 meters (8.2 feet). The basin was filled with water cooled by ice. These "freezing and rewarming" experiments were also conducted under the auspices of Dr. Rascher. Prisoners, dressed in full flying outfits, were thrown into the ice-cold water and left there until varying degrees of low body temperatures were achieved. Once the desired temperature was reached, the prisoner would be lifted out and revived by various methods. Very few prisoners survived the experiments.

In a September 10, 1942 interim report on the results of the experiments, Dr. Rascher wrote:

"The experimental subjects were placed in the water dressed in complete flying uniforms, winter or summer combination, and with an aviator's helmet. A lifejacket made of rubber or kapok was used to prevent submerging...Fatalities occurred only when the brain stem and the back of the head were also chilled. Autopsies of such fatal cases always revealed large amounts of free blood, up to a half liter, in the cranial cavity. The heart invariably showed extreme dilation of the right chamber. As soon as the temperature in these experiments reached 28 degrees the experimental subjects were bound to die despite all attempts at resuscitation. During attempts to save severely chilled persons, it was evident that rapid rewarming was in all cases preferable to a slow rewarming because, after removal from the cold water, the body temperature continued to sink rapidly. I think that for this reason we can dispense with the attempt to save intensely chilled subjects by means of animal warmth. Rewarming by animal warmth, animal bodies or women's bodies, would be too slow."[72]

Blaha, who was also forced to assist in the cold-water experiments, described them as follows:

"...The subject was placed in ice cold water and kept there until he was unconscious. Blood was taken from his neck and tested each time his body temperature dropped one degree. This drop was determined by a rectal thermometer. Urine was also periodically tested. Some men stood it as long as 24 – 36 hours. The lowest body temperature reached was 19 degrees centigrade, but most men died at 25 or 26 degrees. When the men were removed from the ice water attempts were made to revive them by artificial sunshine, with hot water, by electro-therapy, or by animal warmth. For this last experiment prostitutes were used, and the body of the unconscious man was placed between the bodies of two women. Himmler was present at one such experiment. I could see him from one of the windows in the street between the blocks. I have personally been present at some of these water experiments when Rascher was absent, and I have seen notes and diagrams on them in Rascher's laboratory. About 300 persons were used in these experiments. The majority died. Of those who survived, many became mentally deranged. Those who did not die were sent to invalid blocks and were killed just as were the victims of the air pressure experiments. I know only two who survived, a Yugoslav and a Pole, both of whom are mental cases."[73]

Heinrich Himmler even boasted about the human experimentation, writing to Field Marshal Milch in November 1942:

"This research which deals with the reaction of the human organism at great heights, as well as with manifestations caused by prolonged chilling of the human body in cold water, and similar problems which are of vital importance to the Air Force, in particular, can be performed by us with particular efficiency because I personally assumed the responsibility for supplying asocial individuals and criminals, who only deserve to die, from concentration camps for these experiments."[74]

Airman survival experiments weren't the only medical atrocities performed at Dachau. Professor Claus Schilling was allowed to infect the entire populations of Barracks B and Barracks I and 3 with malaria in order to conduct experiments in the treatment of that disease. Barracks 5 was infected with Tuberculosis. "Other experiments were also made [to patients with] ascites [fluid in the abdomen], furunculosis, enteritis, malaria, sepsis, and other medical issues. For these experiments (Malaria) eight prisoners were infected the first time; the second time twelve (all of them foreign preachers). For Sepsis they used the first time six Jewish prisoners whom they gave an intravenous injection of pus. These injections were made by capo Karl Zimmermann. They all got metastasis and died within fourteen days."[75] The next ten prisoners were given the same injection in the upper leg. One patient formed a rather large intramuscular necrosis, which killed him within a few days. Only a couple got sepsis. Survivors received a similar injection in the other leg or, as an alternative to an injection, an incision was made in the healthy leg and pus was poured directly into open wound. The incision was then closed with stitches. Survivors received another intravenous injection of pus that killed them.

According to eyewitness Blaha, some twelve-hundred Dachau prisoners were used in the disease experiments. About eight hundred of them died during the experimentation. The survivors were all sent to invalid wards where they were killed sometime later.

Perhaps one of the most wicked experiments conducted at Dachau tested the effectiveness of poison bullets:

"On 11 September 1944, in the presence of SS Sturmbannfuehrer Dr. Ding, Dr. Widmann, and the undersigned, experiments with aconite nitrate bullets were carried out on five persons who had been sentenced to death. The caliber of the bullets used was 7.65 millimeters, and they were filled with poison in crystal form. Each subject of the experiment received one shot in the upper part of the left thigh, while in a horizontal position. In the case of two persons, the bullets passed clean through the upper part of the thigh. Even later no effect from the poison could be seen. These two subjects were therefore rejected...

The symptoms shown by the three condemned persons were surprisingly the same. At first, nothing special was noticeable. After 20 to 25 minutes, a disturbance of the motor nerves and a light flow of saliva began, but both stopped again. After 40 to 44 minutes, a strong flow of saliva appeared. The poisoned persons swallowed frequently; later the flow of saliva is so strong that it can no longer be controlled by swallowing. Foamy saliva flows from the mouth. Then a sensation of choking and vomiting starts.

At the same time there was pronounced nausea. One of the poisoned persons tried in vain to vomit. In order to succeed he put four fingers of his hand, up to the main joint, right into his mouth. In spite of this, no vomiting occurred. His face became quite red.

The faces of the other two subjects were already pale at an early stage. Other symptoms were the same. Later on, the disturbances of the motor nerves increased so much that the persons threw themselves up and down, rolled their eyes, and made aimless movements with their hands and arms. At last the disturbances subsided, the pupils were enlarged to the maximum, the condemned lay still. Rectal cramps and loss of urine was observed in one of them. Death occurred 121, 123, and 129 minutes after they were shot."[76]

Finally, whether or not Dachau was used as a euthanasia camp is a question that has long been debated. For years some have denied the existence of gas chambers at the camp, and the debate still rages more than seventy-five years later. Yet, there is compelling evidence to suggest the possibility that prisoners were indeed gassed at Dachau.

The first evidentiary example is the construction of the new crematorium at the camp. The original crematorium was a small wooden building with only one oven. It was replaced with a new building constructed with the slave labor of Polish priests held captive at Dachau. The new building, referred to as "building X," was built in a secluded area completely surrounded by trees . A nearly seven feet high wall further hid the building from view. Building X contained four large ovens and only prisoners carrying in corpses of fellow prisoners were allowed near the facility. Sometime in 1944 or 1945, Dr. Rascher, himself, and his wife, were condemned to death for trying to pass off as their own, two children they had taken into their house, an offense known as child substitution. While on death row, Rascher was held at Dachau where he told "fellow prisoner, a British officer named S. Payne-Best, about the difficulties encountered by the SS in camouflaging the gas chamber and concealing the gassings."[77]

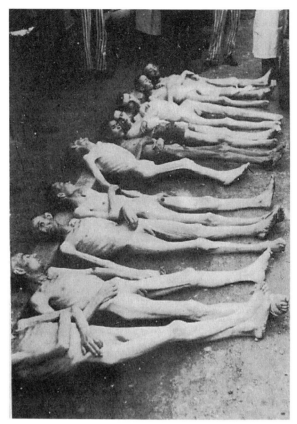

A line of emaciated bodies discovered by liberators at Dachau.
(Source: Report on the Liberation of Dachau.)

Additional proof was discovered when, following liberation, an American war correspondent visiting the facility on May 3, 1945, took video footage showing the detail of the interior rooms of the crematorium. They included:

"the room called the morgue, the room with the four crematory ovens, and finally the gas chamber. This last was a windowless room; metal strips pierced with holes had been set into the concrete ceiling; on one of the iron doors was the inscription: 'Showers.' On the left side of the building were four little disinfestation rooms, also closed with iron doors, which bore the inscription, under

48

a death's-head: 'Attention! Gas! Danger of Death. Do Not Open.'"[78]

Finally, investigators for a U.S. Military Court investigating forty SS men accused of committing crimes at Dachau discovered a "report from a French military mission, entitled "Chemical Warfare," which had been drawn up in May and included a description of the premises."[79] One witness was called at the trial, Dr. Frantisek Blaha, who declared:

> "that experimental gassings had taken place in the Dachau gas chamber. He said that Dr. Rascher,...had once taken him to the crematorium sometime in 1944. Inside the gas chamber, which Rascher himself did not want to enter, Dr. Blaha had to examine people who had been the subjects of an experiment...He said he had seen seven people in the gas chamber; two who were dead, two who had lost consciousness, and three who were sitting normally."[80]

Some of the details provided by Dr. Blaha about the number of people and their conditions changed during subsequent testimonies, however.

In the twelve years that Dachau operated as a concentration camp, hundreds of thousands of men, women, and children were enslaved, tortured, and killed in either the main camp or one of its satellites. It should be noted, however, that not all the Nazi guards brutalized prisoners. In fact, only about five percent of them participated in such brutalities. Some even had the courage to openly oppose the torture and murder that they witnessed. Those guards were placed in "protective custody." Because some of the guards sympathized with the prisoners, the SS required that guard duty be rotated every three weeks. Only the most brutal guards were assigned to permanent positions at the camp. Among the most feared SS Officers were Wäckerle, Erpsmüller, Dr. Frank, Steinbrenner, Heini Straus, Hofmann, and Kantschuster. Unfortunately, these men enjoyed the support of leading members of the Nazi Party including Heinrich Himmler, Commander of the Special Police, and General von Epp, Bavarian Minister of the Interior, both of whom visited Dachau often.

Chapter 6

Dachau – The Death Camp of Catholics

As noted by *Dachau & the SS* author Christopher Dillon, there was nothing special about the location of the Nazis' first concentration camp other than it had been a vacant and available factory premises. The early Dachau, in concept if not location, was founded primarily as a response to the civil war and the postwar violence in Munich. Its gates opened on March 22, 1933, and the camp was initially run by the Kempten auxiliary police, who were commanded by Hilmar Wäckerle. Educated at a conservative officers' school of the Bavarian Army, Wäckerle served Germany on the Western Front at the conclusion of World War I in 1918. He joined the Nazi Party (NSDAP) in 1922 and proudly held the Blood Order badge given to members who joined the Party before the Munich Putsch.

The majority of the earliest prisoners at Dachau were members of the Bavarian and German Communist Party (KPD) and Wäckerle's police did not try to disguise their contempt for Communist sympathizers. Wäckerle, in fact, "felt empowered to murder under the rubric of revolutionary justice."[81] By sometime in April, Wäckerle was named the first commandant of the Dachau Concentration Camp, referred to by many as the Dachau Death Camp. His status as the highest-ranking officer probably had more to do with his assignment to lead the camp than his understanding of the camp's ultimate purpose, though he did have a sadistic streak about him and demonstrated his ruthlessness in the execution of various prisoners.

50

Many gruesome executions were carried out under Wäckerle's direction. One of the first was an amputee by the name of Nefzger. Nefzger, who had lost a leg in World War I, and had been passing sensitive information onto both the police and his brother, a member of the KPD. On May 25, 1933, two guards, Walter Kaune and Szustak visited Nefzger in his cell and beat him savagely. Szustak then motioned with his finger for the legless man to move toward him. Placing his hand on the wall for balance, the beaten prisoner hopped toward the guard. As Nefzger approached Szustak, the guard knocked him off his feet, took a piece of cord from his pocket, and wrapped it around the prisoner's neck. As he struggled to loosen the grip of the rope, one of the two guards took a table knife and three times cut Nefzger's wrist with lacerations that penetrated the wrist to the bone. Finally, the guards hung the dying man using his prosthetic leg. It appears that Nefzger bled to death before succumbing to strangulation.

There were many similar executions attributed to Wäckerle and his men, twenty-two in all. Each murder was premeditated, and each was intended to "both punish the internal dissidents and advertise the unflinching loyalty of the perpetrators on both an individual and collective level."[82]

Wäckerle was extremely interested in getting retribution on the German Communist Party (KPD) in general, but it was Hans Beimler with whom Wäckerle became obsessed. Beimler was chairman of a local chapter of the KPD in Nymphenburg, a suburb of Munich, and was present at the Dachau ammunitions factory in 1919 when his Red Army of the Munich Soviet "Raterepublik" experienced one of their few victories over the right-wing Freikorps. Wäckerle maintained that both the culmination of the German Revolution (aka the November Revolution) that enabled the Weimer Republic, as well as the heinous crime of ruthlessly torturing the hostages in the Luitpold Gymnasium, was Beimler's responsibility and vowed to fire the shot that would kill him.

Wäckerle was so obsessed with Beimler that he even kept a "collection of photographs of murdered hostages from the Luitpold-Gymnasium, with evidence of gruesome mutilation."[83] He believed that he needed no justification to execute his promise to murder Beimler as he held that "a unilateral declaration of revolutionary martial law in the

Dachau concentration camp legitimated summary execution...His 'special regulations' for Dachau included provisions for a 'camp court' empowered to sentence inmates to death, possibly inspired by the rolling courts martial (Feldgericht) used in the counter-revolutionary terror of 1919."[84]

In February 1933, Beimler spoke to a crowd at the last public meeting of the KPD in Munich invoking the battle cry, "We shall all meet again at Dachau!"[85] During that meeting he urged the crowd to resist the growing threat of Nazism. As soon as Hitler assumed power, the Nazis began rounding up KPD members in and around Germany. When they eventually arrested Beimler and his wife on April 9, 1933, just two weeks after the opening of the former ammunitions factory as the Dachau Concentration Camp, Wäckerle hoped Beimler's prescient battle cry would become reality.

Beimler and his KPD colleagues were first subjected to a savage round of beatings at the Munich police praesidium on EttstraBe. Then they were transported to Dachau, where the SS guards reminded Beimler of his battle cry of 1919. Beimler understood that time in the camp would result in certain death. That was certainly the plan of the SS guards who shared Wäckerle's sentiments toward Beimler. To the misfortune of Wäckerle, Dachau was being closely watched by German prosecutors, who were planning indictments for the brutal murders that had taken place at the camp early on, before Hitler thought to exempt camp activities from jurisdiction of the German prosecutors.

Knowing he didn't have much time, Beimler began plotting his escape almost as soon as he arrived. His opportunity came on May 9, 1933. On that night Beimler carefully unscrewed a wooden board that covered his cell window. After crawling through the window, he used the board as insulation when he forced a gap in the electrified barbed-wire fence. He crept rather deliberately along the ground until he reached the six-foot six-inch-high perimeter wall and scaled it without attracting the attention of the SS guards whose focus at the time was directed outward rather than inward. Adding insult to injury, Beimler's escape sealed the fate of Wäckerle, who was promptly replaced as the Dachau's commandant.

By June 1933, Theodor Eicke was named the second commandant of Dachau. He immediately prepared a set of regulations governing the camp's daily operation. The rules were brutal and promised swift and sure punishment for any prisoner accused of breaking them. Those punishment ranged from brutal beatings for inattention to the rules to immediate execution for those espousing political views or caught trying to escape. There was no defense allowed, no trial, no conversation, just brutal beatings and execution. So effective were these regulations in keeping the prisoners in line that they would become the blueprint for the operation of all Nazi concentration camps in Germany.

As previously noted, the Dachau camp was initially used primarily as a facility to house German Communists, Social Democrats, trade unionists, and other political opponents of the Third Reich. By 1938 the purpose of Dachau had shifted from a camp intended to hold and murder Communists and other political prisoners opposed to the Nazi Regime, to a camp expected to facilitate the odious acts of exterminating the Jews, and detaining and torturing Catholic clergymen. In November 1938, more than ten-thousand male Jews were being held at Dachau. They were eventually joined by almost two-thousand Catholic priests. Yet even that was expanded in 1939 and beyond to include Jehovah's Witnesses, Roma (Gypsies), and homosexuals. In 1940, a decision was made to group most Catholic clergymen in Dachau, and five-hundred-twenty-five more arrived from Mauthausen on December 14 of that year. Though the camp reserved two separate barracks for priests, the first Catholic Mass was not allowed until January 21, 1941, and that privilege was suspended in one of the two barracks in September of that year. On October 30, 1941, four-hundred eighty-seven Catholic priests arrived at Dachau from Poland, and in the summer of 1944, French priests arrived at Dachau in great numbers.

On April 26, when the Nazis realized that American forces would soon liberate the camp, the German SS forced more than seven-thousand Jews and some German Catholic priests on one of the infamous German death marches, this one from Dachau to Tegernsee. During these marches many prisoners died of hunger, exposure, or exhaustion. Those who did not die, but simply couldn't march on, were shot to death.

When the U.S. Army arrived at camp on April 29, 1945, more than sixty-five thousand prisoners, were registered at Dachau. This number included thousands of Catholics and almost three-thousand Catholic clergymen. They also discovered "more than 30 railroad cars filled with decomposed bodies, as well as corpses laying unburied around the camp and many sick prisoners....[In all,] the number of prisoners incarcerated in Dachau between 1933 and 1945 exceeded 188,000. [Because of the volumes of camp records destroyed by the Nazis,] it is unlikely that the total number of victims who died in Dachau will ever be known."[86]

Part III

Chapter 7

"Yes, we should strive for unity, but our unity should be based on the truths of our faith as found in Sacred Scripture and the constant Tradition of the Church. No one should want to be united on the path to perdition."
-Bishop Thomas Paprocki of Springfield, Illinois

Catholic Reaction to Germany's Nazi Party and the Nazi Party's Reaction to Catholic Resistance

That Adolf Hitler hated the Jews and used his SS guard to torture and kill at least six million of them in his quest to exterminate the Jewish population from Germany and, eventually, from the face of the earth, is a well-accepted fact of history. Less universalized, however, is the contempt that Hitler and his SS henchmen had for those of Christian faith in general and of Catholic faith in particular.

As an astute politician, Hitler knew that a predominantly Christian German population, one-third of which was Catholic, would not support an open attitude of disdain for Christian people including those of the Catholic faith. He also knew that to achieve his long-term objective of creating an Aryan race, he would need a short-term approach that would appear a bit more subtle than an open declaration of war on German Christians.

Consequently, his speeches from the earliest days of his ascent to power actually indicated a support of Christianity and Catholicism. The 1920 "platform of the then-named Deutsche Arbeiterpartei (DAP, the German

Religious Statistics of Germany, 1910 - 1939 [118]

Year	Total Population	Protestant	Roman Catholic	Other (incl. Jews)	Jewish
1910 (a)	64,926,000	39,991,000 (61.6%)	23,821,000 (36.7%)	1,113,000 (1.7%)	615,000 (1.0%)
1925 (b)	62,411,000	40,015,000 (64.1%)	20,193,000 (32.4%)	2,203,000 3.5%	564,000 (0.9%)
1933 (b)	65,218,000	40,865,000 (62.7%)	21,172,000 (32.5%)	3,181,000 (4.8%)	500,000 (0.8%)
1933 (b)	65,218,000	43,696,000 (67.0%)	21,521,940 (33.0%)	Less than 1%	Less than 1%
1939 (b)	69,314,000	42,103,000 (60.8%)	23,024,000 (33.2%)	4,188,000 (6.0%)	222,000 (0.3%)
1939 (c)	79,375,281	42,862,652 (54.0%)	31,750,112 (40.0%)	4,762,517 (6.0%)	None (0%)

a. German Empire borders.
b. Weimar Republic borders, i.e. German state borders of December 31, 1937
c. Nazi Germany borders in May 1939. Official census data.
d. Including gottgläubig at 3.5%, irreligious people at 1.5%, and other faiths at 1.0%.

Workers' Party) announced by Hitler on February 24 in Munich [proclaimed] 'The Party as such defends the viewpoint of a positive Christianity, without however affiliating itself to a specific denomination. It combats the Judeo-materialistic spirit domestically and abroad and is convinced that a lasting restoration of our people can succeed only from within, based on the principle: the general interest comes before the particular interest."[88]

The final words of point 24 of the platform, as noted above, bears a strong resemblance to the words of the atheist Friedrich Nietzsche, the German writer and philosopher who wrote extensively on the death of God and the end of religion in modern society. "The individual has been taken so seriously, set up so much as an absolute by Christianity, that he could no longer be sacrificed: but the species survives only by means of human sacrifices,"[89] Nietzsche said. The impact of the writings and utterances of Nietzsche on Hitler's anti-Christian sentiments are unmistakable. Despite his feigned support of Christianity, and though being born Catholic, Hitler "rejected the faith as an adolescent, receiving [the Sacrament of] Confirmation unwillingly and never receiving [any] of the sacraments again after leaving home."[90]

Cardinal Secretary of State Eugenio Pacelli, who upon the death of Pope Pius XI would be elected to serve as Pope Pius XII, is seated at the table with Franz von Papen, Germany's Vice Chancellor, and other Vatican and German dignitaries, on July 20, 1933, to sign the Reichskonkordat, a treaty that would lift the Vatican's prohibition against Catholics joining the Nazi Party. (Photo credit: United States Holocaust Memorial Museum)

The Catholic Church, for its part, opposed Nazism even before Hitler's rise to power because the Church deemed it incompatible with Christian morals. In fact, "under the threat of excommunication, Catholics were forbidden to join the Nazi Party (NSDAP) or its organizations."[91] Hitler, for his part, had a well-established covert plan to destroy Christianity within the Third Reich, a plan that may have even predated his rise to power. His plot, at least as envisioned in his mind, would ultimately be accomplished through control and subversion of the churches. His radical vision was to destroy the "Jewish roots of the Christian religion by promoting a Germanic church to replace the 'Jewish church' that had gone astray."[92] If he couldn't execute his strategy immediately, his strategy would certainly be implemented after the war.

Though the Church expressed its opposition to Nazism, many Catholics in Germany, as a result of Hitler's deceit, supported the Führer and recognized in him an opportunity to stop the more immediate evils of Communism and socialism. In that regard, the Nazi party was an ally of the Catholic Church. The Church itself eventually relented, and on July 20, 1933, entered into a treaty with the emergent Nazi nation. Cardinal Secretary of State Eugenio Pacelli, who would later become Pope Pius XII, signed the agreement of behalf of Pope Pius XI, and Franz von Papen, Germany's Vice Chancellor, signed for German President Paul von Hindenburg. This treaty, known as the *Reichskonkordat*, officially lifted the ban on Catholics joining the Nazi Party.

The peace between the Vatican and the German Nazi Party would not last too long, however. In 1937, the eyes of Pope Pius XI were opened to the full range of issues propagated by the Nazi regime. Consequently, despite the feelings of some German Catholics who still supported Hitler, the Catholic pontiff composed an encyclical titled, *Mit Brennender Sorge*. Written in German rather than the traditional Latin, the encyclical condemned Nazi ideology. Two Nazi programs were specifically worthy of condemnation, he wrote; "the policy directed against religious influence upon education and Nazi elevation of race. [The Pope] planned to issue another encyclical, *Humani Generis Unitas*, further criticizing these actions."[93] However, at the time of his death on February 10, 1939, the document remained in draft form.

Despite the pre-emption of the second encyclical, the Catholic faithful began to oppose some of the radical actions of Germany's Nazi Party.

Specifically, it was the euthanasia program, led by Clemens von Galan, which caused the Catholic resistance. So intense was their disapproval that the Nazi party actually paused the program in 1941, but only temporarily. The Nazi anti-Semitism, on the other hand, did not engender the same level of disapproval of the Catholic people in Germany as did the euthanasia of the German people. Only occasionally did they openly and actively voice their opposition to the murder of German Jews. Bishop Konrad von Preysing of Berlin, and his assistant, Bernhard Lichtenberg were the most vocal critics of the maltreatment of German Jews, and their vocal opposition began as early as 1938. Bishop von Preysing petitioned Pope Pius XII to plead on behalf of the German Jews facing deportation, but the pontiff didn't think it advisable to do so. Regardless, Lichtenberg continued to pray for the Jews openly for the next five years. In 1943, Lichtenberg was arrested by the SS for his defiance and died on his way to Dachau.

The official position of the Catholic Church certainly presented a thorn in the side of Nazism. Perhaps equally annoying to Hitler and his Nazi regime were the attitudes of the rank-and-file members of the clergy throughout Germany. Initially, the Nazi SS was content with the use of coercive legal measures, systematic harassment, targeted arrests, and an occasional act of violence to reduce any signs of hostility from the German clergy. By 1940, however, even "the slightest hint of defiance toward the regime led to immediate sanctions – and for many it led to Dachau."[94] Between 1940 and 1945, the number of German clergymen who served time or died in Dachau totaled four-hundred and forty-seven, a number surpassed only by Polish clergymen.

The Gestapo wasn't overly particular about the reason used to execute the arrest of priests. Pretty much any reason would suffice, such as ownership of a previously banned book; any sign of religious proselytism; clippings taken from an opinionated newspaper; or even a personal letter critical of the Nazi Party or its officials. Certain SS guards kept dossiers of priests for years looking for justification for an arrest even if those reasons were inconsistent.

Father Heinrich Hennen served as assistant pastor at the Holy Spirit Church in Münster. He was arrested on November 20, 1941 for the heinous crime of declaring "in a sermon that there was no longer any objective book on Church history. Father Gustav Gorsmann, dean in Gellenbeck in the

Diocese of Osnabruck, was sent to Dachau on October 3, 1941 for having spoken to French prisoners."[95] At the time of his arrest, Father Hennen was already well known to the Gestapo because he had previously posted a card at the rectory entrance suggesting agreeting of "Gruss Gott," translated, "May God Greet You," the equivalent of "Good Day" rather than the obligatory salute of "Heil Hitler." Father Ludwig Braun, from a parish in Freyung am Wald in the Diocese of Passau, was arrested on January 15, 1942 and shipped to Dachau "for 'defeatism,' because he had expressed the opinion in a conversation that the front could be weakened by the enemy."[96] Father Anton Lenferding from Frankfurt am Main in the Diocese of Limburg, committed the grievous offense of abiding by Catholic doctrine in his refusal to perform the wedding of a woman who was divorced. Unfortunately for Father Lenferding, the woman was a member of the Nazi Party.

In addition to the pseudo-reasons noted above, other reasons frequently cited in the arrest records of German priests included illicit pastoral care for Germans or foreigners; inciting children against the State; conduct detrimental to the interests of the State; harboring deserters; being a friend of a Jew; protesting against the marriage law established by the State, and being an eternal enemy of Germany. In fact, "all dimensions of parish activity were scrutinized by the Gestapo and its swarms of informers in the parishes"[97] in an attempt to increase the number of cleric arrests. Their efforts were successful.

In the early to mid-1940s, clergymen were rounded up from every nation that had fallen under the control of Nazi Germany. Initially, aside from the German priests, a majority of the cleric deportations to concentration camps were from Belgium, the Netherlands, Luxemburg and Alsace-Lorraine. They were arrested primarily for "actions and positions deemed hostile to the Reich."[98] Later, however, as German invasions resulted in the capture of additional nations, the incarcerated priests hailed from the occupied countries of Yugoslavia, Italy, and the balance of France. At that point in time, the primary reason for the arrest of priests shifted to "resistance or support for partisans."[99]

Sixty-three of the priests who began arriving at Dachau in 1941 were Dutch. Many of them had been arrested for what previously may have been considered innocuous speech. Among them were Father Peter Van Genuchten, who was arrested for the distribution to his congregation of a pastoral letter that condemned the Dutch National Socialists, and Father

Johann Himmelreich, who spoke to his congregation of the hypothetical Jewish ancestry of Adolf Hitler.

Perhaps the best-known priest arrested during this time was a short and frail man by the name of Father Titus Brandsma. Brandsma was both a Carmelite and a journalist. He was also the rector of the Catholic University of Nijmegan in the Netherlands. Most important, he was a very early opponent of Nazism who rebelled against the anti-Semitic policies, particularly the ones responsible for the dismissal of Jews from schools and universities. If that wasn't fodder enough for the Gestapo, Brandsma used his clout with the Netherlands' Catholic press to publish a thundering commentary calling on journalists to reject all interference of the occupying forces in their publications. "The hour has passed for Catholic Journalists to shilly-shally. They would be disobeying their Archbishop and their conscience if they lent their support to these ideas and to this movement,' he wrote in December 1941."[100]

Less than one month later, Father Brandsma was arrested in the monastery of Doddendaal and slated for eventual transport to Dachau. He arrived at the camp on June 19, 1941 and was dead by July 26, having been euthanized by lethal injection.

The priests of Belgium suffered a similar fate for actively resisting or even for simply offering intellectual resistance. Among the Belgian priests rounded up was Father Leo de Coninck. He was the superior of the Jesuits in Brussels. He was also a professor at the University of Louvain. He curried disfavor with the regime by "having given conferences to the clergy during priestly retreats, setting forth in a synthesis of Nazism: the reasons for its seductive influence on many, the fundamental incompatibility of its doctrine with the Gospel, and the best ways of combating it."[101]

For this most egregious offense against Germany, Father de Coninck was arrested in October 1941, sentenced to time in Dachau, and deported to the camp, arriving on June 18, 1942. He didn't lose sight of his ecclesiastical responsibilities while in prison, however. He became one of the most resplendent voices in camp, preaching the Good News and living the Gospel day after day. Father de Coninck survived his stay in Dachau, saying it represented, "three years of experiences that I would not have missed for anything in the world."[102]

Priest in Dachau – Statistical Chart[103]

Nation of Origin	Number of Clergy Deported to Dachau from 1938-1944	Number of Clergy Released from Dachau before Liberation in 1945	Number of Priests Who Died at Dachau from 1938-1945	Number of Priests Liberated by US Allied Forces in 1945
Germany	447	208	94	45
Poland	1,780	78	868	830
France	156	5	10	137
Czechoslovakia	109	1	24	74
Dutch	63	10	17	36
Belgium	46	1	9	33
Italy	28	0	1	26
Luxemburg	16	2	6	8
Yugoslavia	50	2	4	38
Other	25	7	1	13
Total	**2,720**	**314**	**1,034**	**1,240**

*In addition to the categories represented on the chart, approximately one-hundred and thirty-two clergymen were also transferred from Dachau to another camp or were otherwise liquidated.

In addition to the approximately four-hundred priests from Germany and the seventeen-hundred-and-eighty from Poland, about fifty clergymen were sent to Dachau from Yugoslavia, including Serbian Orthodox, Croatian, and Slovenian Catholics. Twenty-eight was the number of priests deported from Italy, and one-hundred fifty-six priests were deported from France and sent to Dachau.

The tiny nation of Luxembourg, one of the smallest countries in Europe, ranking 167th in size of all the 194 independent countries, was not spared the iron rod of Hitler's SS. Bordered by France, Belgium, and Germany, the people of Luxembourg were primarily Catholic with a spattering of Protestants throughout. Despite its small size, sixteen priests were arrested in Luxembourg and deported to Dachau. Among them was Father Jean Bernard. From 1934 to 1940, Bernard served as secretary general of the International Catholic Office for Cinema (Office Catholique International de Cinema, OCIC). He exhibited an openly hostile attitude toward the German occupying forces. For defending his principled beliefs, he was arrested by the Gestapo in February 1941.

While thousands were transferred, thousands of other Catholic priests were never transferred to Dachau. There is at least one whose story is worthy of recount. He was a Polish priest imprisoned in Auschwitz and is perhaps one of the most famous interned Catholic prisoners in World War II history. His name was Raymond Kolbe, but he is better known to the world as Saint Maximilian Maria Kolbe. His narrative is extraordinary though he didn't live long enough to join his fellow Catholic Poles in Dachau.

Raymond was born in 1884 in the Kingdom of Poland to Julius and Maria Kolbe. They were very devout Catholics with an intense devotion to the Blessed Mother. When Raymond was just ten years old, he prayed to the Virgin Mary for a sign as to what kind of man he would be. Mary appeared to him later that night and offered him two crowns; a white one symbolizing virginity and a red crown signifying martyrdom. Mary asked the boy if he would be willing to accept either crown. "I choose both," the child answered.

Following the apparition, Kolbe's whole demeanor was changed. The once-boisterous boy became "less playful, but increasingly joyful as he came to realize his mission and calling."[104] In 1910 Kolbe entered the Franciscan novitiate and, as a reminder that he was dying to his old self and becoming a new man, was given the name Maximilian Maria. Eight years later, Maximilian was ordained a priest in the Franciscan Order. To combat the errors of Freemasonry, he founded the Militia of the Immaculata (MI) in 1917, a year before he took his final vows. In 1927, he was gifted a six-acre parcel of land west of Warsaw on which he undertook his work. He called his tiny town Niepokalanow, translated the City of the Immaculata. Upon arrival of the Franciscans to the new land, the Polish people helped construct small huts, a seminary, a chapel, and printing facilities. Though modest in stature, the printing facilities were "spectacular in intention as this was meant to be the headquarters to win the world's souls for Christ through Mary."[105]

Kolbe quickly undertook several initiatives to promote his cause and met with uncanny success. Between 1917 and 1939, the organization grew from seven members to five-hundred thousand. He began to publish a magazine called *Knight of the Immaculata*, which had a publication run of about one million. He produced a radio show, and wrote pamphlets and books, all of which had a profound impact in Poland.

In 1938, Father Kolbe intuitively knew that the Nazis would soon invade and capture Poland and as the German army approached a year later, Kolbe sent away almost all of his friars, though he stayed behind with about thirty-six others. Together, the Franciscan friars continued to publish material critical of the Nazi regime even as the sound of approaching army boots grew louder with each passing day. For his actions against the Third Reich, Kolbe was arrested on February 17, 1941 and sent to Auschwitz a short time later on May 28, 1941.

While at the death camp, Kolbe, like all Catholic priests specifically targeted by the SS for cruel treatment, was handled particularly harshly. Despite having suffered from tuberculosis for more than twenty years, he was ordered to carry wooden logs on his shoulders. One day, in his weakened condition, he collapsed under the weight of the load and was brutally beaten by the guards, who gleefully administered fifty lashes. When the beating concluded, the guards picked up Kolbe's near lifeless body and tossed him into the woods to die. But Kolbe did not die. He instead was "carried to the infirmary where, in clear violation of Nazi regulations, he heard confessions of the sick and suffering. The survivors at Auschwitz later attested to Kolbe's tender love for his fellow prisoners and his generosity, which even included giving away the tiny portions of soup and food allotted to him."[106]

In July 1941, a solitary prisoner managed to successfully escape the camp. The Nazi remedy for such insurrection was swift and sure. With all the prisoners standing in the square at attention, a German SS officer by the name of Karl Fritsch randomly selected ten men who would be starved to death in the bunker. One of those selected was Franciszek Gajowniczek, who pleaded for his life saying that he had a wife and children. In an unsurpassed act of courage, Father Kolbe stepped from the ranks saying, "I am a Catholic Priest. I want to die for that man; I am old; he has a wife and children."[107]

Without hesitation Fritsch agreed to the exchange. The ten men were stripped naked and thrown into the bunker where they were deprived of food and water until each suffered a torturous death. Generally, in such cases, there are cries of anguish and sorrow from those destined for such a fate and those cries could be heard outside the bunker to the delight of the SS. To the guards' chagrin, however, there were no such pleadings from Kolbe or the other nine prisoners. Kolbe instead led the men in prayer reciting the rosary over and over again and singing songs to Mary, the Queen of Heaven and Earth. Kolbe was once asked if he thought he might love Mary too much, to which he responded, "Never be afraid of loving the Blessed Virgin too much. You can never love Her more than Jesus did."[108]

Now, as Kolbe and the others lay dying, they offered their last breath to Her adoration. One at a time, each man succumbed to the horrible death of starvation and dehydration, but not Kolbe. He was now wearing the crown that was offered him some four decades prior, and with the other nine lifeless bodies being removed one at a time from the bunker, Kolbe continued to raise a solitary voice in song in honor of his Immaculate Queen.

For two weeks the Nazi guards endured his musical praise when finally, they had had enough. On August 14, 1941, the day before the Feast of the Assumption of Mary, Kolbe was injected with a fatal dose of phenol.

Some ten weeks later, on October 30, 1941, four-hundred and eighty-seven Polish Catholic priests were rounded up from the various death camps and transported to Dachau where more than twenty-seven hundred Catholic priests would be housed in just two barracks intended for only one-hundred-and-fifty prisoners each. Kolbe, however, was not among them. Rather, "while Catholics across the world celebrated Mary's entrance in Heaven, Father Maximilian Maria Kolbe had entered Heaven himself, and this time, he would celebrate [the feast day] with his Heavenly Mother in person."[109]

Chapter 8

The Arrest and Imprisonment of Fr. Jean Bernard

Stadtgrund and Trier Prisons

Monday, January 6, 1941 began as an ordinary day for Father Jean Bernard. A wintery chill spread across Luxembourg at sunrise as the thermometer registered only 17 degrees. Fr. Bernard recited his orders as he readied for his day and prepared to say Mass. The SS had other plans for him, however. Before the day was over, Fr. Bernard was arrested and found himself in the beginning of an ordeal that would change him and many other Catholic priests forever.

Jean Bernard, born in 1907, was the sixth of ten children of a prominent merchant family in Luxembourg. After studying philosophy and theology at the University of Louvain in Belgium and at the Catholic seminary in Luxembourg, he was ordained to the priesthood on about August 6, 1933.

From 1929, Fr. Bernard got involved with work of the Catholic Church on films and cinema. In 1934, he was appointed general secretary of the International Catholic Cinema Office in Brussels. In June 1940 his office was raided by the SS who seized the files, closed the office, and used the premises as a headquarters for the German military police. Eventually, Fr. Bernard's private chapel was converted to a torture chamber used by the SS in its interrogations.

Just six months later, on January 6, 1941, Fr. Bernard found himself confined to the Stadtgrund Prison. He had no idea why he was the target of arrest, though he learned during his interrogation that he was being "accused of having incited the returning Luxembourg citizens with separatist propaganda on various occasions, and carrying letters and messages on his trips between Luxembourg and France."[110] The priest knew that wasn't the case and presumed that the real reason for his arrest might have had more to do with the Gestapo's wanting to take advantage of yet another opportunity to remove a somewhat popular figure from public life in an attempt to break the Luxembourgers' will to resist. For many years Luxembourg priests had been the target of the SS because they were regarded "with some justification, as one of the centers of patriotic resistance for the population, the vast majority of which was devoutly Catholic."[111] The Nazis did, after all, consider Fr. Bernard's Cinema Office the "Vatican's headquarters in the fight against German films."[112] One thing seems relatively clear. If there was any evidence of Fr. Bernard's guilt in that regard, then his case would have been handled by the courts and would have resulted in a prison sentence.

Regardless, Fr. Bernard now sat in a prison cell in Stadtgrund where he was paid very little heed until about three weeks later. The calendar had just turned to February when, at a most unusual hour, the priest was taken in a rather courteous manner to the office of prison superintendent Hardegen. At first the superintendent spoke to him in a fatherly tone as he tried to cajole information from the priest. "I was just in Paris, where I had a few words with your pals Stoffels and Wampach. The two of them have confessed everything, and now they're trying to pin all the blame on you." The clergyman knew that his fellow priests would never do such a thing and he wasn't buying into any of it. It didn't take long, therefore, for Hardegen's frustration to grow, and soon that hostility was apparent in the demeanor of both men.

"Let's get this over with," Fr. Bernard suggested as Hardegen's face contorted into an ugly expression. The two adjusted themselves in their chairs, and Fr. Bernard could feel the blood drain from his face. That's when Hardegen dropped all pretenses. "What is your position on the German occupation of Luxembourg?" "I accept the repeated promises of the Führer to respect the sovereignty of our country," Fr. Bernard replied. The answer clearly upset the superintendent who yelled, "That's enough." They both knew the prisoner had not won. "Pack your things," Hardegen instructed.

Feeling mixed emotions about leaving his newly acquired prison friends, Fr. Bernard hastily packed his few belongings and was escorted to the courtyard where the superintendent's own car awaited. Hardegen personally drove the priest to Trier, using the opportunity to fill the clergyman's head with talk of a German victory that would enable the Nazi regime to rule the world and destroy the Church.

The arrival at Trier prison was relatively uneventful, but the stay would be an opportunity for Fr. Bernard to make some new friends. As soon as he entered his cell, Fr. Bernard could hear the prison chatter as each inmate used chinks in the wall or heating ducts to ask who the new prisoner was. It turned out that the prisoner in the next cell was a Communist sympathizer by the name of Bernard Zénon, but it wasn't until the next morning's shower that the two prisoners had the chance to meet face to face. Immediately thereafter, however, Fr. Bernard was escorted to solitary confinement, which was located on another floor. He never had the chance to develop a friendship with him.

In early April, following the intervention of the prison chaplain, Fr. Bernard obtained permission to say Mass in his cell. For him, this was momentous because it meant that he could have, not only the sacrament, but the sacramentals – his Bible, Breviary, rosary – everything would be available in his cell. This new reality ranked the next few weeks among the happiest of his life. As he began the Mass, his cell neighbor heard him and tapped on the cell wall separating the two inmates. "I'd like to say the responses," the man said, "Would you raise your voice a bit to say the prayers? And please knock three times before the consecration." As Fr. Bernard was performing the Mass, his cell door opened, once again interrupting him. A guard cautiously entered and whispered, "I'm a Catholic." He stayed for a while before rushing out at the sound of approaching footsteps in the corridor.

In prison, the inmates had a way of conversing to keep abreast of the news of the latest arrivals. Fr. Bernard called it the prison telephone. They would simply pass word of an arrival from cell to cell until the very last prisoner in the row heard the news. On one particular day, two new inmates arrived. Fr. Bernard would later learn that they were Father Stoffels and Father Wampach, co-heads of Paris's Luxembourg Mission. On a chance meeting, the clergymen passed by each other in the hall. Fr. Bernard quickly whispered, "Was Hardegen in Paris?" "Yes, and he tried to make us believe you had spilled the beans." Their respective smiles were all the follow-up discussion that was needed.

On another day, Fr. Bernard was warned about the man in the cell across from Bernard's by a prisoner forced into service as a repairman. The cell door opened, and a guard shoved a man armed with some tools into the priest's cell. The man asked if this was the cell where the window wouldn't close. As the guard closed the door and departed, but before a surprised Fr. Bernard could say a word, the inmate pulled some tools from his bag and began hammering the window frame. "The new fellow across from you is a Gestapo spy. He speaks a Luxembourg dialect and is supposed to sound you out." Father Bernard thanked him, as the man knocked on the door to alert the guard. The cell door opened, and the repairman notified the guard that the window was fixed. The guard pulled him out of the cell, closing the door behind him and leaving Father Bernard alone again to continue celebrating his Mass.

After being incarcerated for several months, Fr. Bernard was allowed a single visitor. His mother looked pale and tired when she entered his cell. She gave him updates on his brothers, sisters, and friends, but never spoke about herself. She also brought a significant number of treats, which the guard pretended not to see. As her allotted visiting time had expired, she simply stood, held her head high and walked out. In recalling the story sometime later, Father Bernard indicated his gratitude that his mother didn't cry as this was the last time that he ever saw her.

On May 5, 1941, a guard entered Fr. Bernard's cell at 4:00 AM, ordering the priest to "get ready at once! You're being moved," the guard informed him. "Where?" Fr. Bernard asked, but his question went unanswered. Once downstairs, however, as the priest signed out, the guard quietly pointed with his index finger to Fr. Bernard's next destination – Dachau.

The train to Dachau stopped at every prison along the way, making the trip a grueling thirteen days long. Each night the prisoners were unloaded into a different prison with between ten and twenty men stuffed into a single cell.

Arriving at Dachau

On May 19, the train finally arrived at the Dachau station. Fr. Bernard was the last to exit, and he did so to the sound of a very large and probably tired SS officer exclaiming, "Well, the Lord be praised." Without giving it a thought, the priest replied, "Forever and ever, amen." The others within earshot were clearly amused by the guard being put in his place, but the guard quietly grew red-faced. By the time Fr. Bernard finally got around to looking at the guard of whom he had unwittingly made a fool, the SS officer wore a vicious look upon his face, making the clergyman regret opening his mouth. The guard proceeded to beat the stunned priest to within an inch of his life.

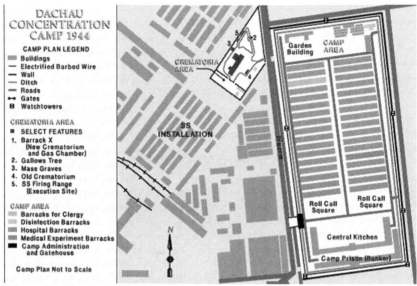

Schematic of Dachau. (Photo credit: United States Holocaust Memorial Museum)

Fr. Bernard and other prisoners were then loaded into a car with hermetically sealed windows. About fifteen minutes later, the car came to a stop and the passengers exited with the help of kicks and curses leveled by the guards. It was clear to all that the prisoners were no longer contained within the state prison system, but rather were now in the custody of the SS, men known for their ruthlessness and hatred. The new arrivals were marched in orderly fashion through the compound; past the administrative buildings; across a stone bridge over a deep stream that formed a moat around three sides of the camp; past a high wall with barbed wire strung along the top; past a number of watch towers with machine guns protruding in all directions; and into an enormous assembly yard. "Eleven new prisoners," one guard yelled out. Confused, tired, and worn, the eleven tried to fit in as best as possible.

A short time later, it was time for the evening roll call. Hundreds of prisoners, dressed in their blue-and-white-striped jackets, trousers, and matching cap, were lined up in columns according to height. Each row contained about one-hundred and fifty-men and the rows were formed very straight. Fr. Bernard still wore his cassock and Roman hat.

Dachau - 1945 (Source:Report on the Liberation of Dachau)

This drew the immediate attention of the commandant, who apparently choose not to issue a beating for the odd dress. After marching across the yard, the prisoners removed their caps and rolled their eyes to the right as the SS guard yelled that there were 12,436 prisoners present and accounted for!

While most men returned to the barracks, the new arrivals were summoned for processing. The men were told to strip naked, and their clothes, and all within the pockets, were taken from them as each was subjected to the routine welcome process. They were shaved with dull blades from head to toe and pushed into a huge shower room. The SS men turned the water on as first scalding and then freezing water rained down. Fr. Bernard summoned all his strength to show no reaction, but others screamed and jumped out of the shower room to the guards' delight. The guards shoved them back in, and this game of cat and mouse continued until the guards grew tired of their sadistic diversion. After this humiliating and painful process, the prisoners were instructed to pick ill-fitted clothes from the pile. Each took a blue-and-white striped shirt, with matching jacket and trousers. They were also given socks and wooden clogs with a cloth or leather top.

Each of the new prisoners was then examined inside and out. The result was jotted down by a guard before each man was told to sit for a photograph. The first man was just finishing this process when he leapt to his feet screaming. "The chair had "a spring-mounted spike in it as thick as a man's finger – a little private joke on the part of the SS photographer."[113] Even something as simple as being photographed was sadistically tainted in this sick house of horrors. As the men were told to march together to the newcomers' block, they learned that the clogs that were issued wouldn't stay on their feet without painfully curling their toes with each step.

In newcomers' block an SS guard inspected the group, saying sarcastically, "There's a priest in this group! Guess which one it is!"[114] His words were followed by a hard slap across Father Bernard's face, causing raucous laughter on the part of the guard. After a few seconds, all the other prisoners joined in the joviality.

The priest and the other newcomers were quite hungry as they hadn't eaten all day. But supper had long since passed. It was now "lights out," and the men were told to retreat to their bunks. For Father Bernard and the other ten newcomers, food would have to wait.

The bunk room where the prisoners slept and the day room where they ate their rations were separate rooms, each measuring about thirty feet long. The bunk room consisted of rough wooden frames connecting a row of bunks stacked three high. There was no actual mattress, rather every bunk had a sack filled with straw that served as a faux mattress as well as a wedge that was used as a pillow. The sheet was real, however, and covered the straw. That was topped with a blanket made of wool, which fit into a washable casing. Of course, there were more men stuffed into a barrack than there were bunks, so the new men had to double up, sleeping head to toe. Fr. Bernard was assigned a top tier, and he wasted no time climbing up. He could tell from the sky-blue triangle patch sewn onto the jacket and trousers of his bunkmate that the man was from the Saar region, but before he could wish him a good night, the man was asleep.

The limited hours of his first day had ended with only a few kicks, one slap, an excruciatingly painful shower, a humiliating grooming, and no food. As he tried to get what he imagined would be some much-needed rest, Father Bernard knew, without reservation, that he had entered a new world and that here the rules would be different. "Here you have to get used to things and adapt, accept the rough camp life whole-heartedly and, as someone put it, become 'an old hand' as quickly as possible," he later wrote in his memoir. "No looking back, no regrets, just dive in headfirst. Do the drill, toughen up!"[115] With that thought, and the help of some prayers, he drifted off to sleep his first night in the new world.

The slumber didn't last long, however, and the men were awakened with a jolt when an SS man entered the barrack. Everyone remained completely still as he flipped a switch that illuminated the barracks. Many thoughts swirled in Father Bernard's mind about the meaning of the intrusion when a most recognizable voice called out, "The man with the egg coddler, come forward!" The priest knew immediately that the term 'egg coddler' was a reference to his clerical hat. "Here!" he called out in a loud voice. "Get down," the guard ordered. As soon as Father Bernard swung his legs over the side of the bunk, he was violently pulled down past the other bunks. "Are you the person with the egg coddler?" the guard commanded. "Yes," the priest responded. His answer was greeted with a painful jab to the ribs. "Here you say, 'Sir, yes sir!'" "Sir, yes sir," Father Bernard replied, not wanting to repeat the rib jab. "Priests are filthy swine! What are you?" "A filthy swine, sir!" the priest answered obediently. The answer must have caught the SS officer by surprise. Perhaps he wasn't expecting it. "Carry on!" was all he said as he left the room. Father Bernard lifted himself back into his bunk and covered himself with a blanket. Only then did he explain the "Lord be praised" story from earlier in the day to his neighbor. "He's out to get you," the man said, adding, "We call him 'B.B.' It stands for 'blond beast.'"[116]

The morning routine was equally as nerve wracking as were the late-night visits from the SS. The men were jarred out of their bunks promptly at 4:00 AM when the klaxon, an excessively loud electronic horn, similar in sound to that of a "modern-day tornado warning siren," pierced the tranquility of slumber. The inmates referred to it as "the bear." The lights simultaneously flared up, and everyone jumped from his respective bunk, making their way to the washroom while still lingering in a semi-conscious state. The washrooms had two large circular basins with several flexible shower heads. There was also a stone trough in which inmates could wash their feet. Because of the overcrowding, prisoners had to push their way to the shower and trough in order to wash. Soap was an unavailable commodity.

Once the prisoners had washed, the bunks had to be made, not simply thrown together. Fitting a round sack of straw into a perfect rectangle was no easy feat, but the men pulled out hidden boards and

> "pieces of wood cut to exactly the right size for this purpose. One prisoner would insert a stick through a slit in the sack to stir up the straw and push it toward the edges, while his mate pressed back with a flat piece of wood to make the edges straight. Carefully they stretched the sheet over the now square sack to make four very precise ninety-degree angles. Then the cover was folded to a width of 60 centimeters (a measuring stick was available for this purpose) and placed on top so that the lower edge was 20 centimeters from the end of the bunk, and the cover stretched flat the entire length of the bed, rose at right angle at the pillow and then was laid flat on the pillow again. The fold in the blanket had to run exactly parallel to the blue and white stripes of the casing. Besides the straight edges required on the straw sacks, the most important part was to get the 'waterfall' right, meaning the place where the cover must ascend vertically at the pillow like a step in a staircase. Finally, since there were ten three-tiered frames lined up, side-by-side, the height of each made bed had to precisely match that of all the others at its level."[117]

The entire drill seemed to Father Bernard an exercise for the mindless, but a misstep could easily result in a severe beating depending upon the mood of the SS guard.

The morning coffee routine was equal folly. Two insulated pails were used to fetch the morning brew. Two prisoners carried the empty pails to the kitchen, filled them with coffee and then attempted to carry the heavy pails back without spilling anything. There were no handles on the pails, so they were carried by the side and bottom of the pale, making the effort to avoid spillage very difficult. Of course, at Dachau, no prisoner could walk, but rather were required to jog everywhere. Additionally, the entire excursion was timed, so if one took too long, there wasn't much time left to actually drink the coffee. To add to the misery, the new prisoners had not yet been issued the aluminum mugs and their names were not yet added to the list for the kitchen staff, meaning that in addition to not being able to drink the morning coffee, they wouldn't get any bread at lunchtime. For the men who hadn't eaten in the past twenty-four hours, that was not good news.

The prisoners were barely back in the barrack from the coffee run when the klaxon sounded yet again. Someone yelled to fall in for a head count, and immediately lines of men formed between the barracks. Each prisoner marched in precise order until they reached the assembly yard. The newcomers were counted separately as they were yet to be schooled in the art of marching or singing, nor had they been given any work assignments. Consequently, they were lined up on the barrack street between their barrack block and the next one. An SS guard appeared from nowhere and counted the columns. When the counting ended, the men were forced to remain standing at attention in the pouring rain for about forty-five minutes. The rain felt quite chilly on Father Bernard's newly shaven head, but these are not the type of things that anyone complained about. "It's always like this," a fellow inmate explained, "we're at eighteen hundred feet here, and at this elevation in Bavaria there's usually a stiff breeze."[118]

Once the other squads were marched off to work, a guard returned to allow the new prisoners back into the day room of their barrack where the capo, Hugo Gutmann, was required to ask the prisoners questions and record their information. He started by giving each man a hard slap in the face. "You have to get used to that boys," he says, "I know what I'm talking about. Half the camp has passed through my hands. A lot of them have me to thank for it that they're still alive."[119] As Camp capos go, Father Bernard didn't think Gutmann was too unlikable, "he just hit a lot."[120]

Aside from hitting, Gutmann explained to the new prisoners exactly how Dachau Camp was run. "The prisoners are responsible for the daily routine. The SS [were] there just as overseers and supervisors, and to administer beatings whenever something [went] wrong. At the top of the pyramid was the head prisoner for the whole camp. He [had] thirty 'barrack heads' under him, and each of them [supervised] four 'room heads,' since each barrack [contained] four rooms.'[121]

Gutmann informed the inmates that they would remain with him for about three or four weeks. Once he felt they were ready, they would be assigned to a barrack. Father Bernard would be in one of the two priests' barracks. "You don't have to work," he told the priest, "Your food is better, and you get to take afternoon naps. You can pray all day long and there's a daily ration of wine."[122] Father Bernard received that news with mixed emotions. While the agenda sounded reasonable, why would his "collar" be used to segregate him from the general population who would suffer much more? Before he could ponder the question too deeply, he received a swift kick to the ass at the same time he heard Gutmann's instruction to leave.

Father Bernard was just entering the latrine when he heard the voice of the Blond Beast ask the capo about the "egg coddler." He quickly dropped his trousers and took his seat on one of five toilets hoping to avoid another beating, knowing full well that someone else would catch the beating on his behalf. Fear has a way of compromising a person that way. "Gone to interrogation, sir!" he hears Gutmann respond, and just like that, B.B, perhaps a bit disappointed that he was unable to brutalize the priest, left the room. That's how quickly fortunes could change at Dachau.

In those first couple of days, Father Bernard was given two white cloth strips, each about six inches in length. Both strips were imprinted in black with the number 25487. He also received two triangles of bright red. Each side of these was about four inches. His instructions were to "sew them on, now!"[123] From viewing other prisoners, Fr. Bernard knew that they were to be affixed to the left side of the jacket and the right side of the trousers. He wasted no time beginning that assignment making sure that both the jacket and the patch were smooth with thee point of the triangle facing straight down while the other end was exactly parallel to the number strip above it. Achieving this type of precision was not easy, and Father Bernard sweat profusely thinking about the type of beating that might be administered if he didn't do it exactly right. He was further distracted thinking about the significance of his assigned number. With roughly twelve-thousand inmates at Dachau, even if some were released, the number indicated that some ten-thousand camp inmates had died. He queried another inmate about it and was told that after reaching a certain number, camp administrators started numbering from the beginning again. They had started over several times already.

Mealtime was not something an inmate was likely to write home about. Four men split a single loaf of bread weighing about three pounds, unless you were a priest, then your loaf was split with only two others. That news didn't sit well with Father Bernard. He and his fellow priests quickly split a loaf into four portions, saving the final portion for a new arrival who had not yet been allotted bread. They were quickly informed, however, that their act of generosity would mean little in the scheme of things. "Look, there are over a thousand members of the clergy in the camp right now – nearly one prisoner in ten. Potentially it could have a huge influence, especially with so many Poles here. That's why they put the priests in separate barracks, and it's also why they get 'better treatment. The idea is to make the other prisoners hate them and keep them morally isolated as well."[124] Father Bernard instinctively knew that his fellow inmate was right.

New arrivals were frequent, and one was even from Luxembourg. But none had a familiar face. There was one very friendly arrival, however. Father Heinrich Zöhren was a Capuchin priest who showed up one day to take the new inmates outside to march, run, do 'up-and-down exercises,' and sing. He seemed to get along rather well with Gutmann, and Father Bernard also took an immediate liking to him. Cappy, as he was called, introduced himself and then let the men out the door. The last man out was assisted by a strong kick from Gutmann.

The next order of business for the new arrivals was a singing lesson. All inmates were required to sing German songs as they marched or worked, and they were expected, required in fact, to know all the words. The song for that day was Madagascar, but for the unfortunate Poles who had just arrived by transport, the songs were in a foreign language, and they didn't understand what they were singing. The lesson was interrupted with the frightened cry that B.B was on his way. He rode his bicycle to an open window and climbed in. Studying every mouth, the Blonde Beast noticed that the Pole standing aside Father Bernard was moving his lips but only pretending to sing. B.B. grabbed the poker from the stove and used it to 'beat time' on the poor man's shaved head. It took only a couple of blows for blood to start spurting out of the man's head. Father Bernard kept his own face buried in the songbook when he was suddenly filled with rage. He wanted to lash at B.B.'s throat, but either fear or common sense prevented him from acting. He did manage to look up and stare at the monster and he suddenly had a new appreciation for the word sadistic. Father Bernard's reaction was not unnoticed by B.B., however, and the SS guard burst out laughing. "Ah, the gentleman feels like rebelling, does he? Well, Well! We've met before!"[125] Then, grabbing the priest by the waist, B.B. picked him up and tossed him into an unfortunate Pole. Both men slammed against a cupboard that tipped over backward. From his position on the floor, Fr. Bernard didn't move a muscle, but sensed a large boot positioned directly over his head. Rather than slam it down upon the priest's head, however, he yelled for the singing to resume. As it did, B.B. disappeared out of the same window from which he had arrived.

Joining the Priests' Barracks
Day 1 - June 2, 1941

The first two weeks had gone by, and Father Bernard was now ready to relocate to the priests' barracks. He and Cappy were two of the five priests assigned for the move that day, the second of June. Packing was easy. Aside from a single set of camp clothes which he wore, his belongings consisted of only a song pamphlet, a pencil, and two handkerchiefs.

Gutmann assigned another prisoner to escort the inmates. Although priests were housed in three separate clergy blocks in the main camp; 26, 28 and 30, Father Bernard was led to barrack 26, which, much to his delight, was the same barrack to which Cappy was assigned. They entered to the eerie sight of about sixty prisoners sitting upright and motionless around eight tables. The barrack was identical in setup to the one just vacated. A large stove covered in green tiles occupied the center of the room, which had two long sides, each comprised almost exclusively of windows. The shorter walls were filled with open storage lockers, five units per side.

The jolt of the frozen scene was surreal. Father Bernard noticed the division immediately. Around one table sat eight Protestant ministers, but it was the only table at which there was an empty seat. He hesitated but was rather quickly nudged to that seat much to the obvious displeasure of the table's other occupants. "Is it always so crowded here?" Father Bernard asked, hoping to break the tension. "Shut up," the room's head prisoner yelled, "Do you think you can do whatever you want just because Good Friday is past?"[126]

Exhibit of a prisoner hanging by his arms
at the Dachau Concentration Camp Memorial Site

Later, while marching to get their lunch, Father Bernard learned the meaning of the "Good Friday" reference. On Good Friday 1940, the SS found a pretext to punish about sixty priests by hanging them on the tree for an hour. The "tree," he was told is really a pole and the description of the hanging left Father Bernard speechless. The hands of each priest were tied together behind their back with palms facing out and fingers pointed backward. The hands were then turned inward, and a chain was tied around the prisoner's wrists. From that chain, the priest was hoisted up the pole. The joints of each victim were twisted and torn apart by the man's own weight. Throughout much of the following year, and certainly throughout the entirety of Lent, the SS psychologically tortured the priests, telling them at every opportunity that the same punishment would be inflicted on this Good Friday as well. According to Father Brunke, a Franciscan friar from Hamburg who was paired with Father Bernard in the lunch parade,

> "Lent was awful. We hardly dared to breathe, so we wouldn't give them even the slightest excuse. Several of the priests who were hung up last year never recovered and died. If you don't have a strong heart, you don't survive it. Many have a permanently crippled hand."[127]

The "kitchen exercise" was orderly and rapid. That was a requirement lest another beating be administered. Because the priests were assigned no work detail, they had the responsibility of fetching meals for every barrack and returning the empty pails to the kitchen. It was the only work they did, morning, noon, and night, so it was not something that most would complain about. There was an art to successfully accomplishing the objective, however, and Father Bernard learned that lesson rather quickly, albeit the hard way.

Most men were sliding their feet as if on ice skates, but Father Bernard wasn't aware of the incredibly slippery, wet flagstone floor on which his wooden clogs found no traction. With an audible thud he fell to the floor. Fortunately, the sound was heard only by those around him, and not by the SS who would have used the opportunity to administer a vicious beating. The surrounding prisoners lifted him to his feet immediately, sparing him the pain.

As the line continued forward, the men split into two columns, one column moving on either side of a long row of pails with sharp metal handles. Each pail had a number written in chalk indicating the barrack to which it belonged. Father Bernard reached for a bucket emblazoned with the number "10," but as he tried to lift it, found it to be terribly heavy. Looking around, he noticed that others were wrapping their hats around the handle of the bucket. He did the same as he lifted his pail off the counter. Father Brunke positioned himself on the opposite side and the two set off for the door, carefully gliding so as not to repeat the fall that marked

Father Bernard's grand entrance. A new arrival directly in front of them, however, was not so lucky. He fell and was savagely beaten by the SS as he lay on the floor. Though it was their instinct to help the poor fellow up, they dared not interfere with the SS men. Consequently, with bowed heads, they continued past him and made their way out of the kitchen. Once outside, the two lowered the pail to the ground and switched sides to relieve the pain in their hands. As they did so, another prisoner slipped down the steps behind them, spilling hot soup all over himself. Though he was severely burned, another very hungry priest reacted most unsympathetically, saying with obvious disgust, "It's one of the pails for us!"[128] Hunger, as the veteran prisoners knew, can be a difficult suffering to charitably endure.

While the other prisoners of the camp were served red cabbage soup, the priests were given a much more satisfying pea soup. That was just one more wedge that the SS put between the priests and the general population. Each priest was given about a quart of soup as well as three or four boiled potatoes, although some of the potatoes were rotten as Father Bernard realized when he inspected his lunch. He quickly discarded one of his rotten spuds, but to his surprise, one of the other inmates suffering from extreme hunger quickly gobbled it up. The daily ration seemed sufficient to a newly arrived inmate who was still drawing energy from his own body stores, but Father Bernard would soon enough experience the pangs of real hunger.

The post-meal routine was equally arduous, but if the schedule of cleanliness wasn't maintained, the penalty was severe. The mental timer was turned on, and inmates scrambled for a space at the trough. After several minutes of scrubbing, too long a time if everyone was to get a turn at the sink, Father Bernard realized that he was not able to get his bowl inspection-proof clean. There was apparently an artificial fat in the soup, and the cold water that poured from the sink's faucet was simply not sufficient to cut through it. In fact, the reaction to the cold water actually caused the fat to congeal on the bowl. Other inmates, accustomed to the routine, used a scrap of newspaper to rub the inside of the bowl to heat it up. The warmth helped to melt the grease, and the newspaper soaked it up. But Father Bernard had no scrap of newspaper to call his own. Few inmates did. Those unfortunate souls had to devise a different method of producing a bowl clean enough to pass inspection. Some did, but some could not. Once the inside of the bowl was considered sufficiently clean, a needle was used to scrape out anything that may have been stuck between the bowl's handle and rim. Those whose bowl was deemed "dirty" were reported to the SS by the Capo. Even the placement of the bowl on the light-colored wood shelf was controlled. It had to be placed on the shelf with the handle pointed forward, but an inmate was not allowed to slide the bowl into place for fear that it might leave a mark on the wooden shelf. It had to be set down carefully and with the utmost of care, equidistant to the bowls on either side of it.

The prisoners in priest barracks were also required to take an afternoon nap, but rather than messing up the bunks, which are so difficult to remake, Father Bernard's bunk-mate informed him that it was better to settle onto hard boards exposed in the gap between two straw sacks in the corner of the bunk frame. While uncomfortable, it certainly was preferable to the beating that might ensue from a hastily made bunk following nap time. Not every prisoner had this option, but Father Bernard and his bunkmate were quartered in a fairly inaccessible corner of the room out of view of the capo. Once in the bunk, however, Father Bernard found it was nearly impossible to sleep, due to all the disturbances that took place during that hour.

Even before the end of the hourlong nap time, there was an audible call of "WINE DETAIL." Twelve men quickly rolled from their bunks without getting dressed. Though a clear violation of the rules, some thought it preferable to the senseless beating issued to the last man ready. The beds were made in a panic, but Father Bernard had no need to worry about that chore despite being one of the twelve. He instead used the time to help a half-blind elderly professor from a seminary in Cracow with the chore. After a final hasty inspection, they all hurried into the day room, grabbed their tin cups, and took a seat at the table while Father Bernard and the other eleven fetched the wine.

The wine detail distributed the bottles of wine to their fellow clergymen. Generally, an afternoon glass of wine might be a welcome pleasure, but in Dachau it was simply another horrible stress. First, the men listened in awkward silence anxiously awaiting the screams that would come from the other room; someone whose bed was poorly made, perhaps a priest who was inadequately dressed, or even just the victim of his own lack of speed in accomplishing those tasks. Then the call of "ATTENTION" as the SS guard entered the room. The SS was always present for the wine detail adding to the pressure of the situation. The men leapt to their feet in unison and remained motionless. The "OPEN THE BOTTLE" order was given, and the prisoners quickly passed around the only two corkscrews provided until all twenty bottles were opened.

There was so much anxiety among the prisoners that nothing went smoothly, requiring the capo to curse and punch the slackers. The capo would never shirk his duties in front of the SS for fear of being severely beaten himself. Before the blows had ended the "POUR" order was shouted out. The tins of three men were filled from a single bottle. Each cup evenly filled, or a punishment would be bestowed upon the man who was pouring. After a quick inspection by the guard and the capo, the prisoners were given the "DRINK UP" order, generally followed by a crude remark such as, "YOU STINKING PADRES." That's when the SS officer would take a position on a chair, providing a birds-eye view of all the priests. He did this to identify anyone who might not be drinking fast enough. The wine was to be drunk in a single gulp, and the empty cups then turned upside down above the priest's head to prove it was empty. One clergyman choked and was unable to drink. The SS guard flew from his chair and hovered over the man in an instant. He hit the bottom of the cup with his fist so violently that the metal rim sliced a semi-circle through the priest's lips and cheeks coming to rest at the bone. Blood squirted everywhere, and the priest was carried off to the infirmary.

When wine-time was over, the remaining men were ordered back to their bunks to complete the final ten minutes of their "hourlong" nap. This fruitless exercise required that the beds be made yet again, the third time that day, and the day was not yet half over. Because of the nap, wine drinking, and other extraordinary handling afforded the priests, a Protestant minister attacked the Catholic pope accusing him of petitioning through diplomatic channels for the clergy to be given special treatment, adding, "I hope it ends soon."[129] Another Catholic priest confirmed the pope's intercession to Father Bernard who still had mixed feelings about the entire matter.

When evening finally arrived, everyone was ordered to bed early, even before the annoying sound of the klaxon. The capo was asleep in the day room and apparently wasn't bothered by what happened next. From the far corner of the bunk room a voice quietly began summarizing the day's military and political news, first in Polish, then in German. Reading from various newspapers that had somehow been obtained, he also added his own personal commentary. The entire event was very risky, and the others simply folded their hands and sat quietly.

A blessing was bestowed upon the priests by the Monsignor Cozal, Bishop of Leslau. Even the Protestants joined in, making the sign of the cross. For Father Bernard, and many others, the blessing gave "meaning to our suffering, [lifted] it above the purely human and [joined] our small, personal suffering to the sea of injury and persecution that the church of Christ [endured] and must endure. His blessing [let] us share in the graces and comforts and [provided a source] of strength that fed the first martyrs. O miracle of the communion of saints, which became our experience here! Even our sleep is illuminated by the great certainty: *Et non prevalebunt* . . . And the gates of Hell shall not prevail against it."[130]

Day 2 - June 3, 1941

Priests at Dachau were awakened before dawn at 3:45 AM, a full hour earlier than the other prisoners at camp. After shaking the straw from their still naked bodies, they put on their striped trousers, jacket, and hat to make the trek to the kitchen to get the coffee. Washing had to wait until after the beds were made and the lockers straightened, and then, only if there was time, might they get the luxury of a quick wash. In this system of internment, Father Bernard was learning, hygiene was less important than the daily regimen, which was even crazier in the priests' barracks than it had been in the newcomers block.

Once those tasks were accomplished the prisoners were pushed out of the barrack so the rooms could be cleaned. The morning air was pretty cold, and the men shivered as they tried to peer through the windows to observe Emil's inspection. Emil, like most capos, was a communist. That was not a coincidence, but rather a product of their longevity at camp, since most of the early Nazi arrests were of communists. Some of them had been in camp for five years, long enough to have been relatively dehumanized or at least left devoid of any compassion toward their fellow man. Emil was no exception. He was a monster, even more so than those in charge of the other two clergy barracks. They were driven by a desire to keep their jobs, which came with several perks. Capos "were allowed more food and more frequent use of the camp shop. They didn't have to join work details and were real kings in the camp. On the other hand, if the men of a room or a barrack attracted the attention of the SS for sloppy marching or singing, for instance, then the head prisoner was the first to be hanged or flogged – 25 lashes on his bare back with the double bull-whip."[131] Consequently, if a prisoner's name was called, the capo would pull that prisoner's bed apart or empty the entire contents of his locker into the street. That process generally resulted in a few bloody heads, docked meals or worse, a report to the SS. It was only after inspection was complete that the men were able to breathe a sigh of relief and relax a bit.

The morning head count followed the barrack inspection, and the prisoners were required to march in rows of ten. The capo called out the selected marching song, which on Father Bernard's second day in priest barrack 26 was *Hazelnut*! Prisoners were required to begin at the same time and on key under the threat of punishment that included an hour's worth of exercises – up-and-downs and running. There might even have been a forfeiture of the midday meal. The headcount was for the entire camp with the three priests' barracks marching last. Barrack 26 had far fewer people than the other two clergy units because only two of the four rooms were being used as bunk rooms. The other two rooms in barrack 26 were used as a chapel and a storeroom. Father Bernard took careful count of the rows of clergy, estimating there were between seven-hundred-fifty and eight-hundred men in them. The drill seemed to last forever, and during that time, the rows had to be perfectly straight to the point where a bullet could be fired between them. The men were required to hold formation for just under an hour despite the weather conditions. Then the orders began in rapid fire. "Caps off," "eyes right," "eyes straight ahead," "caps on." Then finally, dismissal, with the command, "at ease." This exercise was repeated three times a day, every day, even in the most extreme weather.

The Chapel

To a Catholic priest, nothing is more sacred than the seven sacraments of the Church. These include baptism; confirmation; Reconciliation, also called penance or confession; the Eucharist, also called Holy Communion; the anointing of the sick, also known as extreme unction or the last rites; holy orders; and matrimony. Instituted by Christ and imparted to His Church, these sacraments, with the exception of matrimony, were administered in varying degrees by the priests of Dachau. Of these seven, the sacraments most commonly administered were confession and extreme unction. The priests, who confessed to each other, often heard confessions of laymen while walking along a road or working at an assignment. Though forbidden, it was easy because it would appear to the SS or the capo that the men were engaged in meaningless conversation. Extreme unction could also be performed in a stealth way so that it was almost undetectable to the SS guard or capo. Father Maurus Münch recalled his experience with Father Josef Zilliken just prior to Father Zilliken being taken to the infirmary.

> "Before this transfer, all priests of Trier, assembled in the chapel, administered extreme unction to him. With supreme serenity, even facing death, this man reminded me of a patriarch. He received extreme unction with perfect lucidity and conscience, and he embraced all of us before his transport from the chapel to the infirmary. On October 3 he gave up his soul to God."

The sacraments least administered in Dachau were baptism and holy orders. There is only one documented case of each of those sacraments taking place in the camp. Father Rene Fraysse wrote of a "little Jewish boy who had been fortunate to escape from the camp in Auschwitz alive, and who asked to receive baptism."[132] Perhaps the most memorable story of sacramental rite at Dachau involved the priestly ordination of a young seminarian by the name of Karl Leisner. Having attained the stage of deacon, Leisner was to be ordained in 1939, but he was diagnosed with a severe case of tuberculosis and was arrested while still at the sanatorium. Despite the conditions at the camp, which exacerbated his health issues, Leisner was described by those who knew him as even tempered. Even with the hardships of camp life, he always signed his letters home, "Ever Joyful." By 1944, the tenor of the war was shifting, and the German Army was retreating with great regularity, leading to hopes of liberation. It was his disease and not his incarceration that dimmed his chance of ordination. The arrival of Clermont Bishop Gabriel Piguet at Dachau on September 6 changed that outlook. During a discussion with Father Leo de Coninck who argued that a priestly ordination at a concentration camp "would be God's revenge and a sign of victory of the priesthood over Nazism," Bishop Piguet said, "I will not hesitate a moment to perform this ordination."[133] After dealing with the bureaucratic minutia involving the proper permissions, a stunning ordination ceremony, featuring all the required vestments, was performed behind the barbed wire of Dachau, an event certainly unique in Church history.

Of all the Church sacraments, however, perhaps the one most revered is Holy Communion. That is when the faithful receive the Body and Blood of Jesus Christ, the risen Lord. He Himself commanded that this be done at the Last Supper that Jesus shared with his Apostles on Holy Thursday, the evening before He entered into His Passion. The point at which an ordinary wafer and a cup of wine are changed into the Body and Blood of Jesus is known as the Transubstantiation. Only a priest has the power and authority to change bread and wine into such a sacred instrument of salvation and the miracle of this change is brought in the eucharistic prayer by an action of the Holy Spirit. To a priest, and to many Catholic faithful, there may be little as emotionally painful as the deprivation of Holy Communion. The need for the Eucharist to a priest, who has chosen to live in close union with the Lord Jesus, is a basic one. Father Bedřich Hoffmann noted that this need could "only be understood by another priest."[134] Yet, from its opening in 1938, neither attendance at Mass nor reception of Holy Communion were allowed at Dachau or at any of the other concentration camps under the control of the Third Reich.

That changed at Dachau, however, on January 21, 1941, several months before Father Bernard arrived at camp. Beginning on that date, the priests were allowed to attend Mass each day at 4:00 AM in the chapel of barrack 26. On those occasions the wall separating the day room from the bunk room was removed, creating a room measuring approximately 30 feet by 60 feet.

That a chapel even existed at Dachau was a historical anomaly resulting from a very complex series of negotiations begun in January 1940 between apostolic nuncio Cesare Orsenigo and Ernst von Weizäcker, the German Secretary of State for Foreign Affairs. For months neither side would budge from his position, but eventually the Vatican ambassador

Paul F. Caranci

prevailed, and on November 9, 1940, Hanns Kerrl, the Reich's Minister for Ecclesiastical Affairs, sent a letter to Cardinal Bertram, Archbishop of Breslau and president of the German Bishop's Conference, indicating that all the Catholic priests would be regrouped at Dachau and would be allowed to say or assist at Mass in a new chapel that was to be built at the site. On November 13, the nuncio informed Luigi Cardinal Maglione, Secretary of State of the Holy See, of the compromise.

The impact of the decision was immense. "While the priests started coming to Dachau in the month of December, and this resettlement reached its full capacity of 1,007 by the end of the year, the work of setting up the chapel began in the Stube I of Block 26, where the refectory and the dormitory were merged to provide a satisfactory space."[135]

Initially, construction was not hurried, but authorities eventually steadily increased the rate of production allowing for the celebration of the first Mass on January 21, 1941. The accoutrements were quite simple then. A small table served as a makeshift altar. It was covered with a bed sheet and placed against the short wall at the end of the room. A cross was painted on the wall behind the altar and blocks of wood served as stands for two real candles the burned on either end with a crucifix standing between them. There were even tiny fragments of Host on a small plate near the door, which each man took as he entered the chapel. Despite its extended size, the room filled rather quickly, and the men squeezed in until they were standing shoulder to shoulder. A former chaplain in the Polish army, Father Pawel Prabucki, celebrated the first Mass and each Mass on Monday through Friday thereafter. "On Sunday, Mass was celebrated by Bishop Michal Kozal who enjoyed this dispensation thanks to his episcopal status."[136] The required vestments, the hosts, and the altar wine were always gifted by the parish priests in the town of Dachau. Father Prabucki had established a similar setting at the Sachsenhausen concentration camp, from which he had been transferred just six weeks earlier. Being so close to the altar, but still unable to celebrate the Mass personally, was an extreme emotional suffering for the hundreds of other priests imprisoned at Dachau, but they were comforted greatly by the reception of Holy Communion. Consequently, the Vatican diplomats worked indefatigably to ensure a steady supply of hosts and altar wine for the camp chapel. Father de Coninck verified that "hosts and wine were procured for us in abundance by the parish priest in [the town of] Dachau, with whom, on the twenty-fifth of each month, we had regular communication for the needs of our worship."[137]

The chapel was steadily improved over time and, by the occasion of the camp liberation by Allied forces, the Dachau chapel resembled any ordinary chapel on the outside. "A tabernacle was constructed secretly in the carpenter's workshop that served to build furniture for the SS personnel of the camp. Some pieces of tin cut out of cans, and then of brass, made it possible to embellish it with some basic ornamentation. The first altar cross was cut out of rough wood, and the candlesticks were made of materials salvaged in the camp. Over time, thanks to gifts of prayer books from the parishioners in the town of Dachau, and to income from 'the organization,' the liturgical objects and ornaments abounded. The modest cross was replaced by an authentic work of art; stations of the cross and some prints depicting Saint Joseph and the Sacred Heart of Jesus decorated the wall; precious priestly vestments covered the space that served as a sacristy. Nothing was lacking: eventually, one could even find a harmonium for accompanying the choirs during the services."[138] The Dachau chapel, in fact, ended up attaining a real degree of refinement. There was even a choice of monstrance available for exposition of the Blessed Sacrament. One, an ebony cross with a lunette shaped like rays cut from tin, took on a severe, symbolic manifestation.

Photograph of the crude altar crafted in the Chapel at Dachau.
(Photo credit: United States Holocaust Memorial Museum)

The second was constructed from a light lemonwood. One object in particular, a statue of the Blessed Virgin Mary, inspired a great deal of veneration. She was a gift of Auxiliary Bishop Joseph Martin Nathan, of the Archdiocese of Olomouc, and for unknown reasons that might be considered miraculous, the statue was allowed into the camp.

Hardly any of these refinements were available during the time of the first Mass or even during Father Bernard's time at Dachau in 1941 and 1942, but the lack of traditional church fineries didn't matter to those in attendance at that first celebration. They were simply grateful to be given the opportunity to attend Mass and to receive the sacrament of Holy Communion. Regardless of how small the wafer, they all knew that it contained the fullness of Jesus Christ, Body, Blood, Soul, and Divinity.

To Father Bernard, this meant the world. Regardless of the rudimentary nature of the surroundings, he was so overjoyed at the sight of his first Mass that he began to cry. He understood that the gathering was a "comfort and hope and strength for new suffering joyfully accepted."[139]

The priests also knew instinctively that the Mass was tolerated, not graciously allowed by the camp authorities, and they knew equally well that it could be disrupted at any moment, which made the clergymen nervous and uneasy throughout the entire ceremony. The chapel was under the vigilant scrutiny of the SS who watched over its proceedings very carefully. They made sure that the service did not exceed thirty minutes in length, a time limit they imposed on the priests. Like everything else at Dachau, there were severe penalties if the time limit was not adhered to, and a guard paced in front of the chapel to ensure compliance or to report violations.

Father Adam Kozlowiechi, who was arrested in November of 1939 and originally imprisoned at Auschwitz but transferred to Dachau on December 12, 1940, noted, "One day, when Communion lasted longer than the authorized time, a furious SS officer entered the chapel and railed at the celebrant, no doubt Father Prabucki, shouting: "Everyone out and line up! Eat up and have done with it!"[140]

From March until September 1941, priests of any nationality were allowed admittance to the chapel provided they were supervised by Father Prabucki, the de-facto chaplain. Laymen, on the other hand, were never allowed into the chapel. This exclusion was, perhaps, as punitive for those responsible for proclaiming the Gospel of Jesus Christ and administering the sacraments as it was to the faithful who found such great solace through participation in the Holy Mass. Prisoner Fr. Joseph Rovan, alias Pierre Citron, a member of the resistance movement when he was arrested in 1944, wrote about the "priceless consolation" that attending camp Mass offered the priests of Dachau, in his memoir *Contes de Dachau.*

> "The priest was saying the same Latin words that all his confreres, at the same hour, were repeating in their morning Masses throughout the world. No longer could I recall the world of the concentration camp. Each one, for a precious moment, was restored to his original, fragile and indestructible dignity.... On the way out, in the pale light of the early morning, one felt capable of facing a little better the hunger and the fear."[141]

Another camp prisoner, Fr. Marcel Dejean, recorded similar sentiments in his memoir, *Avoir Vingt ans dans les camps nazis: Des Vosages a Flossemburg par Dachau, Auschwitz et autres.*

> "We went to meet...the One who held our lives in His hands; we rediscovered the idea of love in the midst of suffering, hunger, egoism, hatred or indifference, and also a palpable sense of calm: the beauty of the altar, the ornaments, the rites, in the midst of our filth and poverty; tranquility, recollection and solitude in the midst of constant overcrowding and all sorts of noises....The SS were no longer anything but a sad nothingness beside the splendid, immortal reality of Christ."[142]

For many of the priests, the real punishment was inflicted in September 1941 when the SS prevented all priests not of German heritage from assembling in the chapel of barrack 26. At that time Father Prabucki was removed from his chaplain post and replaced by Father Franz Ohnmacht, who was one of the first inmates at Dachau. Father Ohnmacht was arrested from the Austrian Diocese of Linz and brought to Dachau on

June 17, 1938. Though faced with this horrible dilemma of having to shut out his fellow clergymen, he nevertheless chose to obey·the orders from the SS to prevent any non-German priest from even peering through the window of barrack 26.

Faced with deprivation of the Eucharist, some priests resorted to saying Mass in secret and tried to obtain unconsecrated hosts clandestinely. Though bread was available to prisoners, it was leavened bread, and liturgical law very clearly prohibits the consecration of leavened bread for Communion. Liturgical law, in fact, prescribes exactly how the host must be made.

> "The holy eucharistic sacrifice must be celebrated with unleavened bread made of pure wheat and confected recently, so that there is no risk of spoilage, and with natural wine, made of grapes, pure and unspoiled., without admixture of foreign substances."[143]

Further, the "combined presence of the bread and wine was essential in order for the Eucharist to be valid. Considering this twofold imperative, various systems were put in place in order to 'organize' the hosts and the wine."[144]

One of the riskier strategies was executed in the plantation store where the deportees sold some of their goods, such as the beautiful azaleas and gladiolas grown outside the camp, to the SS and the public. The plan was originated in 1944 before the Polish priests were allowed discreet access to the chapel. On May 16 of that year, Josefa Maria Imma Mack, called Mädi for short, entered the store to purchase some fruits and vegetables for the convent in Munich that she planned to enter. While in the store she was approached by a youthful priest from Sudetenland by the name of Father Ferdinand Schönwalder. He asked her to bring some hosts and wine the next time she visited the store so that he and other Polish priests who were not allowed to attend Mass could share it. She agreed, and "very soon Mädi was responsible for bringing seven hundred each week, a task that she accomplished, with conviction and not without risk, until the liberation of the camp."[145]

Father Hoffmann was also a "conspirator" in the acquisition of hosts. In the midsummer, he had managed to gather some ripe ears of wheat while his work commando was passing by a field. Alois Kolacek, Father Hoffmann's friend, dried and crushed the wheat and mixed it with flour to make the hosts. Many priests took untold chances to ensure there would be a supply of consecrated hosts available so that those priests who couldn't enter the chapel would be able to receive the precious Body and Blood of Jesus, even if each clergyman could receive only a tiny fragment of the sacred bread.

Those same priests would then celebrate Mass in secret, much as the early Christians did in the catacombs. The "catacombs" of Dachau were in the bunk room between two bedsteads or in the plantation. The priests were in constant fear of being discovered by the capo or an SS guard, but receiving the Eucharist was worth the risk to them. They used a lid from a box of lozenges as a paten to hold the hosts, a glass as a chalice for the wine, and a handkerchief for an altar linen. In the plantation, the priests hid a miniature altar in the ground. The hosts were consecrated while the priests knelt, so the SS believed they were working the soil. Once they received the Body and Blood, they went back to work. They would always consecrate more hosts than were immediately needed so they would have a supply for other days when they weren't able to "celebrate Mass." Much like those early Christians, the priest used the acronym *ichthus*, the Greek word for "fish," when referring to the Eucharist in the presence of others. The letters of the acronym stand for *Iesous Christos Theou Huios Soter* or *Jesus Christ, Son of God, Savior*. For distribution, the priests would draw a fish on the outside of paper envelopes that contained fragments of the Eucharist, so that other priests would know what the envelope contained. Using this system, the priests were able to deliver the Eucharist to laypeople throughout Dachau, even those confined to the infirmary. Father Jean Kammerer, who was confined to the infirmary following his arrival in Dachau on October 29, 1944, the Feast of Christ the King, wrote:

> "Father Andre Schumacher, of the Diocese of Besancon, succeeded in infiltrating Barrack 19. He brought me a second helping of soup to share and, in a cough drop box, some consecrated hosts. Therefore, I met that evening with the priests of the convoy and with some comrades

The statue of the Virgin Mary that was miraculously allowed to be displayed in the chapel at Dachau. (Photo credit: United States Holocaust Memorial Museum)

who had been found out as practicing Catholics, in a hallway of the bunkhouse where half-light reigned, to receive Communion together."[146]

Father Alexandre Morelli celebrated Midnight Mass on Christmas Day in 1944. He set it up in the consultation room of the Dachau optometrist, who was also a prisoner at the camp. He told the story this way:

"At Dachau I performed the most extraordinary priestly
ministry of my life... One of my greatest blessings was to
be able to celebrate a clandestine Mass for Christmas of
'44... In case of surprise, everything was set up so that I
could immediately make the glass and the host disappear.
And the Mass began. Footsteps of the SS were heard in
the corridor. The steps came closer, passed, returned. It
was very dangerous. Our hearts throbbed as though they
would burst, but we wanted to have our Midnight
Mass."[147]

Father Ohnmacht was released from Dachau on March 16, 1943
and was replaced as chapel chaplain by Father Georg Schelling. Schelling
was also from Austria and had arrived at the camp on May 31, 1938.
Though cautious, Father Schelling was a bit more of a risk taker than
Father Ohnmacht had been, and Schelling tried to create an atmosphere
more accommodating to the Polish priests. By mid to late December 1943,
the number of German clergymen in barrack 26 had diminished, and
priests from other national backgrounds, except the Poles and Lithuanians,
were housed there. By 1944, when an influx of French priests began
arriving, the rules were relaxed even further and Polish priests were once
again allowed to spend a little time in the chapel, albeit very discreetly.
Just prior to liberation, they openly frequented the chapel and celebrated
Mass there.

Those attending the first Mass in January 1941, as previously
noted, were watched very closely by the SS. While they were still giving
thanks, the priests were interrupted with a call of "lice inspection." "How
often are these scenes put on?" Father Bernard inquired of another
prisoner. "In the other barracks, now and then on a Sunday at most. Here,
there's an inspection nearly every day," he responded. "Apparently, the
clergy are more susceptible to lice!"[148]

The inspection process was just another humiliation the priests
had to endure. First, every prisoner was required to strip naked and then
file, one by one, past the capo who was seated on a stool holding a list of
names and a pencil. A particularly thorough search was performed on
certain parts of the body to ensure that there was no trace of lice or scabies.

Occasionally, the capo would invite colleagues from other barracks to attend the performance. Because the prisoners from those barracks were out on work detail, their capo generally had little to do. As each priest approached, the capos would joke, most inappropriately, about the priest's body parts. Father Bernard was still too euphoric about being allowed to attend Mass, however, to have this inspection spoil his day. "We have heaven in our hearts, and the Lord resides next door (in a drawer), in our midst," he thought to himself. Everything would be just fine.

Day two had come to an end.

June Through October 1941

Every other Sunday, the inmates were required to write letters. Those who were Dutch and those from Luxembourg had to write their letters on plain white paper. The Germans and Poles were required to use official camp stationary. The reason was never made clear, but it mattered little to Father Bernard, who drafted his first letter rather hastily. He shared it with a seasoned inmate who crossed out half of it. There was a similar result after review of the second draft from which most of the interesting parts were stricken. The final, approved version was nothing more than a few sentences that indicated he was still alive. All future letters looked just about the same, "Dear Mother, I received your letter. I am well. I'm healthy and in good spirits. I don't need anything. Send me a few stamps and some money for my account here, in case there is something to buy in the camp shop...."[149]

On another day, as the prisoners in barrack 26 were washing dishes, they heard a racket outside the barrack. Hugo Guttman, the capo in newcomers' block, and Emil, the capo of Barrack 26, were beating up a Protestant pastor by the name of Brendt who had the gall to give the Hitler salute. Prisoners were forbidden to do such a thing, and the pastor was paying a price with blood. Brendt was having a difficult time accepting the fact that he had been arrested. He had one son who was killed in the war and another who was a high-ranking SS officer. Brendt kept hoping the he would have been able to save himself with political gestures, but one did not survive Dachau by doing such things.

Shower time was a most competitive venture. There were limited shower hooks on which to hang clothes and too many men were vying for them. The competition began as soon as the men left the barrack carrying only a towel and a bar of soap. As they approached the shower room, which was located near the kitchen, some of the experienced men had already stripped naked in the hopes of grabbing the first available hook. The room itself was designed to hold only three-hundred men requiring several to share a single shower head. The water was typically warm and comforting at first, but that lasted only a few seconds before it was changed to scalding and then to ice cold. Those who jumped out of the way of the cold water were sometimes treated to a spraying of cold water from a hose held by the capo. The rafters above contained giant iron hooks. That was another place in which they hanged the men who were sentenced to a punishment of one or two hours on the "tree." It was also the place where sixty priests were suspended on Good Friday in 1941.

Nothing in Dachau, it seemed, was uneventful. One day, on the return from the shower room, the prisoners failed to sing their song properly. The capo instructed the men to do "up-and-down" exercises until it was time for head count. In the extreme heat, the men began to run, stop and lay flat on their stomachs, stand up and repeat the process. It took no time for the once-refreshed men to lay covered in a layer of dirt and sweat. This is how they remained until the next shower day. In addition to the filth experienced by all, three men fainted from the heat and exhaustion and were taken to the infirmary.

On one occasion, and to the delight of the prisoners in barrack 26, the daily ration of wine was withheld for two consecutive days. On the third day, however, the flow of wine was restored, and the inmates were required to consume all three days' worth in one sitting. That was a bottle of wine each without a break. Most of the men became drunk, causing the SS guards to break out in laughter at the sight of a pack of drunk priests, but at least there were no casualties.

As weeks passed and more men were incarcerated at Dachau, the overcrowding at the camp had become even more pronounced. In response, the administrators decided to convert room four of barrack 26, previously used as a storage room for band instruments, into a bunk room. Father Bernard eagerly volunteered to assist, partially to escape the torment of the room head, but also as a means of passing time more quickly. The head of room four had already been selected, and he was a pretty decent fellow. Father Bernard entertained some hope of transferring into that room upon its completion.

During the time of renovation, the priests received a shipment of breviaries – twelve new volumes in all. Some speculated that the essential prayer books were compliments of the bishop of Fulda, though no one knew with certainty. While the books were proudly displayed on a shelf in barrack 26, no permission had been given from either the SS or the room head to open them. With plenty of time available, however, some priests were predisposed to pray from them anyway, leaving those priests battered and bruised from the resulting beating at the hands of the capo. The breviaries remained on the shelf, unopened from that point. For the priests having them so close without being able to pray from them was, in itself, a form of psychological torture. Later, however, permission was granted for the priests to have their own breviaries if they were received via mail from home.

Father Joseph Knepper, the pastor in Ehleringen, joined the priests of barrack 26. He was also from Luxembourg, a fact that delighted Father Bernard. Knepper's appearance was also cause for a rare but hardy laugh. The extremely tall, thin priest arrived in the barrack donning trousers that were much too short, a shirt that fit him like a short-sleeve shirt, and a cap that fell below his ears. The lightened mood compensated for the otherwise tragic situation that was his incarceration. Knepper was assigned to room four while Father Bernard still remained in room three. Unfortunately, the prisoners of room four had to sleep on bare boards because there were no straw sacks available for them. Regardless, Father Bernard found it oddly comforting to get the latest news about friends and acquaintances from a fellow Luxembourger even if the news came at the cost of Father Knepper's incarceration.

The addition of new prisoners to Dachau also caused a strain on the food supply, and the summer and early fall months brought about an end to the potatoes that were previously enjoyed in the cabbage and carrot soup. The prisoners, who were already experiencing painful hunger every day, quickly learned just how much hungrier they could get.

A second arrival from Luxembourg was assigned to barrack 26, but this time, Father Bernard was able to exert some influence in having him assigned to room three. Pastor Schiltz from Tütingen entered the barrack wearing a cap that was so tight, it puffed out at the top like a baker's hat. Despite his comical appearance, he brought a great deal of news about his parish and before going to sleep, gave an individual blessing to each and every occupant of room three. Father Bernard, as a veteran of the camp, also felt a new sense of purpose, satisfaction, and courage as he took it upon himself to tend to the "greenhorn" of the barrack.

Two days later, Father Schiltz complained of an intense pain in one of his feet. Most of the time, such pains were simply ignored until they went away. This remedy was ineffective on the foot of Father Schiltz, however, and a short time later, it had swelled to a horrific size. By the time permission was obtained for him to visit the infirmary, he had collapsed and was still unconscious when he was carted off. He remained in the infirmary for more than two months.

One of the prisoners' chores was to ensure that the floor remained oiled. Failure to do so would result in the usual beating by the SS or the capo. Oil, however, was seldom available unless the room head were paid. The prisoners often had to pony up some money just to do a chore that, if left undone, would cause them severe pain. Consequently, they paid without complaint.

September brought about the twenty-fifth anniversary of Bishop Cozal's ordination to the priesthood and permission was granted for him to say Mass on that day. The Poles rehearsed their songs while some of the others busied themselves with the task of constructing a monstrance. They had all the materials needed for its construction in some empty tin cans that looked like brass on the inside along with a broomstick and a few flat pieces of wood. The wood formed a multi-layer rectangular base and a piece of the broomstick was inserted in the middle of it forming a stem. The bottom of the can was the capsule, and the sides were artfully cut to form the rays of a sunburst. The work crew had only a hammer, knife and a pair of pliers so the process took about two weeks, but the objective was achieved, and the priests were certain of the Savior's approval.

Early October brought the release of a prisoner. Father Joseph Knepper had only recently arrived, but he was being released. There should have been apparent joy any time a prisoner was released from camp and Father Bernard was certainly happy for his friend, but his loss also left that hollow feeling and a sense that "luck won't be passing so close to you again for a long time."[150] Father Bernard would later learn that Father Knepper's release was not definitive. Still, it took only a few days to fill Father Knepper's bunk. The new prisoner was Dr. Baptiste Esch, a priest from Luxembourg, but everybody called him Batty. He was an editor at the *Luxemburger Wort* and was previously housed in Berlin at Camp Sachsenhausen along with Monsignor Origer, his supervisor. Batty was no stranger to Father Bernard who spoke to him as often as possible with upbeat messages about the Allies advances in the war. Batty was a little less optimistic, not in the Allied Powers ultimate success in the war, but rather in his own future. "Wherever I end up," he told Father Bernard, "everything goes wrong."[151] Father Bernard was quite shaken by his words, realizing that he was indulging in his own illusions and experiencing every bit of suffering, both physical and mental, in its entirety. Such people just aren't destined to make it, and Father Bernard knew that he shouldn't spend too much time with him. Two weeks later, Batty joined Father Bernard in clergy block. Catastrophe struck the very next day.

"Everybody Outside," the head of room three barked. Grabbing what they could the entire barrack emptied out to the street, where stood the camp commandant. They all knew there was trouble brewing. They were joined on short order by the clergy from the other rooms. The head prisoners began to yell and hit anyone within their reach but they too, seemed to be in the dark about the happenings. They shouted out incoherent orders: "Get all your things!" and a moment later, "Leave everything inside!"[152] Father Bernard and the others suspected that there would be a pocket inspection, so they quickly began to "unload all contraband, Rosaries, cigarette ends, toilet paper, rags to wrap our raw feet in..."[153] The Germans and Poles were instructed to line up separately, leading to speculation that they might be gassed. Father Bernard decided to join the ranks of the Poles as did Father Schiltz, Batty, and a Dutch Jesuit by the name of Father Robert Regout. He was a professor from the University of Nijmegen and remained remarkably calm through the ordeal. When the SS officer finally arrived, he began to give orders and counterorders, which kept the men moving about, but also resulted in some swift punishments. Some of the men from barrack 26 were moved to barrack 30 while still others, including Father Bernard, were relocated to barrack 28. The former occupants of those barracks, all Germans, were moved to barrack 28. It appeared that the SS was trying to segregate the German clergy from all others. Perhaps, some reasoned, it was because of the radio speech denouncing the Nazi regime. Or it might have been a response to the German bishops' issuance of a public protest. Regardless of the reasons why, Father Bernard was now separated from the chapel housed in barrack 26.

Camp Commandant Hoffman took a position in front of barrack 28 and addressed the new occupants of that unit with an obscenity-laced and insulting tirade that demeaned priests and revoked the camp privileges that they had previously enjoyed. As the priests entered the barrack, Batty made the mistake of asking the head prisoner if the Luxembourgers could be roomed together. The question earned him a severe blow to the head. Batty never learned the "camp language" and did not realize that capos and room heads were stripped of any emotion after years of camp abuse. Regardless of Hoffman's reaction to Batty's question, Father Bernard, Father Schiltz, and Batty were all assigned room one.

October also saw the arrivals of new priests from other camps. Fathers Joseph Stoffels and Nicolas Wampach, also Luxembourgers, arrived from Buchenwald where they had spent the previous six months. They were from the Congregation of the Priests of the Sacred Heart of Jesus and had been working at the Luxembourg Mission in Paris at the time of their arrests. Father Stoffels, though an optimist at heart, suffered very poor health and was immediately declared unfit for work, which meant that he would not have to carry food pails as would the others. The two of them were also assigned to room one, which meant that five Luxembourgers sat at the same table each day. That was the good news. The bad news was that the influx of prisoners caused the quality of food to decline significantly. The soup, already devoid of potatoes, grew even thinner. And the cravings that plagued the inmates grew in intensity. For Father Bernard, it was sweets that caused him the greatest issues. He craved sugar intensely. But that longing gave Father Bernard a bold idea.

While the letterhead the Poles were provided bore a bold, printed warning against a prisoner receiving packages, the plain paper that he was given had no preprinted message. "Who knows," he said to his friends, "It's possible that if something were mailed to us, they might let us have it. I'm going to risk it."[154]

With that, he included the following message on his next letter home: "How are my bees doing, and how is the honey harvest this year? It's a shame you can't send me a pot of it."[155] The letter must have made it through the censors because ten days later, Father Bernard was summoned to interrogation by the camp commandant. It was highly unusual for any prisoner to hear directly from him and in preparation for the meeting he was given a fresh shave and a clean pair of trousers. The barrack clerk walked him to the administration building, where he took off his shoes as required and waited outside the commandant's office for three hours when finally, he got the call to enter.

"Prisoner 25487, date of birth 8-13-07 reporting, sir!" Father Bernard yelled at the top of his lungs while still standing in the doorway. He stood motionless at attention while the commandant played with his dog, paying no attention to the priest standing before him. Then, picking up a small round package, the commandant hurled it at Father Bernard's head. The priest remained completely still because reacting would probably have warranted a beating. He remained motionless as the package hit him and then rolled to the floor. "What is that?" the commandant commanded. "It must be honey, sir. My mother wrote me that she had sent some," he yelled. "What?" the commandant asked incredulously, "Are you out of your mind? Don't you know that's forbidden?" "Yes, sir," the priest yelled out, "But my mother doesn't, since I'm from Luxembourg and have to write home on plain white stationary." "Pick it up! Dismissed! Write at once and tell them never to send anything again,"[156] the officer demanded.

Father Bernard picked up the package and returned to his barrack where the head prisoner was incredulous that the priest had not been beaten. When the other prisoners spotted the pot of honey that he carried, they looked in stunned silence hoping that they might get a taste. Their desire was satisfied as Father Bernard shared its entire contents with the five men. Before long, there was nothing left. Later, the entire camp received an order to end the next letter home with the words: "We are strictly forbidden to receive any packages."[157]

The following day, the priest block received word that the clergymen would no longer be allowed to drink wine, take a midday nap or attend Mass. There was no German prisoner distribution of the big food kettles either, requiring that the other priests make two trips. Worse, barbed-wire fencing was installed outside of barrack 26 separating the rest of the priests from the chapel. When the German priests in barrack 26 celebrated Mass, the other priests, though unable to cross the barbed-wire barrier, would still watch from outside of the rear chapel windows, but when their activity was discovered, those windows were covered with an opaque white paint. Their breviaries, rosaries, and any other religious article were taken away and any religious activity of any kind was suddenly prohibited.

November Through December 1941

One morning, the barrack head announced that barrack 28 was classified as a working block prohibiting anyone from remaining in the day room during working hours except for barrack personnel. From that day, the priests were banished from their barrack to the outdoors after morning coffee where they were required to march, run, sing, and do "up and down" exercises. This would be the new routine until the midday meal, when the prisoners were able to relax a bit, but the exercise started over again after the midday meal and continued until the evening head count. It didn't matter if it was hot or cold, sunny or raining. That was just how it was going to be.

During the exercise periods, the prisoners were not allowed to put their hands in their pockets, raise the collar on their jackets, or do anything else that might help keep them warm. The head prisoner of barrack 28, a real beast, watched from the window to ensure compliance.

Eventually, work groups were formed requiring anyone with a skill or trade to volunteer. This was a good thing as it enabled the men to get some relief from the routine and get away from the barrack, freeing themselves of the head prisoner and the SS. Work detail also qualified the men for an "extra morning ration" that might consist of large slice of bread spread with margarine or even a piece of sausage. Though most of the priests signed up, none were called as the SS was still reluctant to allow the priests to mingle with the general population for fear that they might evangelize.

November 1, 1941 was the feast of All Saints. It also brought the season's first snowfall. That was most unwelcomed news because the priests were assigned the task of shoveling. Others who had been in camp the previous winter warned them about the strict procedures they were required to follow. The order was issued almost immediately. The men were handed a shovel and a board for scraping. They were also given some wheelbarrows from a stock of about two hundred. The men had to maintain a jogging pace while they shoveled and scraped lest the sun melt some of the snow depriving the sadistic SS of their enjoyment.

The day to which the prisoners looked forward had finally arrived. November 15 was the day that the prisoners exchanged their summer clothes for winter clothes made of a slightly thicker material. They were also anticipating the issuance of socks, coats and perhaps even the gloves that were issued to prisoners in the winter of 1940. By the day of the next snowfall, the anticipated gloves materialized, but not the coats or socks. Needless to say, those who hadn't yet grown accustomed to being in the cold weather with very little clothing for warmth had an exceptionally difficult time adjusting.

The last weeks of 1941 also brought another Luxembourg priest to Dachau. Legendary Pastor Jean Brachmond from Moersdorf arrived and was housed temporarily in the new prisoners' barrack. Nearly everyone had a story about the tricks Pastor Jean used to play on the Germans. This stay at Dachau would certainly provide plenty of time to hear verification from the man himself.

During that same period, Father Stoffels developed an inflammatory skin rash that covered his entire face. Most would not consider this condition luck by any stretch of the imagination, but in Dachau "luck" had its own special definition. Because the condition was highly contagious, Stoffels was carted off to the infirmary where he remained for months. At this stage of the war, prisoners were still provided with reasonable care when infirmed. Being out of sight of the capo, room head and the SS was considered lucky regardless of how it was achieved.

These final weeks also brought about yet another change of barrack. The men of barrack 28 were forced to move into the already overcrowded barrack 30, bringing the total number of prisoners in that barrack to seven hundred. Father Schiltz was assigned to room one while Batty, Wampach and Bernard remained together in room two. Brachmond was ushered to room two, and Father Stoffels was sent to room four as soon as he was released from the infirmary.

If it were possible, life in Dachau got even more miserable following the move. Prisoners were now required to sleep with five men to a single bunk. Father Bernard and Batty snagged a straw mattress and were able to keep it the entire time they were in barrack 30. The day room was converted to add more bunk space, which meant that meals would be consumed either while sitting on the floor or laying in the bunk. On the upside, the bed-making rules were no longer enforced, and bunk inspections were eliminated. Even the housekeeping rules were relaxed during this time. The prisoners in this barrack were given only two very thin blankets per man, so to keep warm at night during the bitter cold, they rolled up in one blanket and placed the other one over both of them.

Batty decided to sign up for a work detail as a means of obtaining an extra food ration, and Father Bernard decided to join him. Eighteen men were to be selected, but more than fifty men marched over to barrack 2 where physical exams were being conducted on the applicants. Batty was selected, but Father Bernard was not. For his lack of good health, he was given a round of kicks and sent back to barrack 30. The work detail was with Transport Commando 2, which was also called the Marsh Express, and required that the men pull and push a heavy truck trailer. Though the tires were inflated, it was still extraordinarily difficult to move. Moving it required two men to pull a shaft from the front, four to push from the back and six men on each side in harnesses attached to the trailer. About six of these trailers were used to transport goods to and from the camp. The workload, however, did not suit Batty, who returned at the end of the day overly exhausted. "It's too late for us," he said one day in his usual pessimistic tone, "We're already too weak to work. The extra ration doesn't make up for the increased effort we have to exert."[158]

Father Bernard did get a taste of the level of exertion required of a work detail when he was punished after a few crumbs of bread were found in his locker. After being called a dirty pig, a piece of filth and other choice names, he was ordered on the Sunday work detail headed for Eyke Square. This large open space was located off campus, in the SS town at the end of a broad avenue where the high-ranking officers kept their villas. The work assignment included sweeping the area and filling small carts with the accumulated debris. The work was not as exhaustive as Batty's assignment, and Father Bernard was able to see civilians for the first time in many months, something from which he derived pleasure. One woman walked by wearing a fur coat and holding her young daughter's hand. He stared at them as his mind wandered and flooded with thoughts.

"Does she know about our misery? Does she really consider us criminals? Or feel any empathy for us at all? And what about the child? The two of them were free. Able go wherever they wanted. [They were probably] on their way to a comfortable home, where they [would] spend Sunday afternoon with daddy, who [had the] day off."[159] Before he could complete his fantasy, he was knocked back into reality by a powerful jab to the ribs courtesy of the SS guard. She's "the wife of the camp commandant," the guard told him. "*She's* allowed to keep her fur coat. *My* wife had to donate her rabbit fur to the clothing drive for soldiers on the eastern front,"[160] he said rather bitterly.

***

The ground outside was frozen and icy, but the prisoners were still required to march rather quickly to fetch the morning coffee. Father Bernard and the other inmates stepped into the blackness of the early morning freeze and fell like dominoes on the ice as their wooden clogs provided no traction at all. In order to carry the heavy pails while marching, the inmates had to remove their clogs and walk along the ice with bare feet. On one occasion, Father Bernard slipped, and his hands were scalded by the hot coffee. The pain was intensified in the cold air, and the burn was severe enough for him to be sent to the infirmary for bandaging.

Fortunately, the heat in the barrack had now been fired up despite the shortage of fuel for the oversized wood stove. But because some of the wood and briquettes needed to be reserved for the evening, the room just never felt too warm.

***

Finally, striped coats and speckled, multi-colored socks were provided. The coats were mostly a patchwork with very little of the original wool remaining. Regardless, they were very welcome additions and provided measurable relief from the extreme cold that arrived very early in the season.

***

Batty returned from work detail one day in early December with news about the war. An SS officer told him that the English recaptured Tobruk. Father Bernard couldn't contain his excitement and rushed to tell his fellow Luxembourgers the great news, saying, "It will go quickly now, you'll see." "Nonsense," Batty replied as he had no optimism left having succumbed to total pessimism. Father Bernard knew that Batty needed an intervention if he were to survive Dachau and that night, when they got into their bunk, he told Batty that he must fight the urge to let everything get him down. Batty would hear none of it, however. "Tobruk may fall, but the war won't be over all that soon. I don't want to sugar-coat the suffering with fairy tales for children."[161] Father Bernard knew that it is belief in just such fairy tales that keep an inmate from falling prey to fear. He also knew that his "friend's bleak attitude would be toxic and destructive"[162] for him too. It appeared to already be taking its toll on Batty's health. Almost without control Father Bernard blurted out, "You don't get along with anyone. It's your own fault if people are turning their backs on you. We *want* to cling to every straw! Every bit of hope is welcome, if it helps me to keep going and feel strong inside, even if the image is a false one, a mirage. You want to play the part of a hero, a tough guy, but you're only making yourself depressed and robbing the rest of us of hope at the same time..."[163]

Father Bernard was exhausted and very close to despair himself when he had finished. The pain of internment at Dachau removed all pretense of tact from his statement. Batty made a comment about being all alone now, but the pity party wasn't moving Father Bernard who said nothing in reply. A wall was now separating the two friends and neither of them had the energy to scale it. Neither of them was able to sleep after the discussion, and the two wept silently. After what seemed a very long time, Batty grabbed Father Bernard's hand firmly. Father Bernard returned the squeeze. "Let's stick together," Batty said quietly. "Yes," Father Bernard replied. That was the only word he could muster up through his exhaustion, but it was enough. The two friends drifted into sleep.

Christmas 1941

Tuesday, December 24 finally arrived, and the prisoners were given permission to stay up a little bit longer than usual to celebrate Christmas Eve. Some of them crafted a pine bough stuck in a tin can and decorated it with two candles. The Polish priests sang rather melancholy tunes and one man belted out the Gloria in splendid fashion. The Polish bishop provided a commentary which Father Bernard barely understood. Shortly thereafter, the prisoners climbed into their bunks feeling rather sad and dreaming of home.

Christmas day, however, was just a mere workday, and Father Bernard was up very early to fetch the coffee, switching assignments with another inmate so that he could deliver a pot to his friend Cappy in barrack 26. He had gotten word that Cappy had something for him and he could hardly wait to find out what it was. Because Cappy was working inside a barbed-wired enclosure the two had to keep a distance, but Father Bernard set the coffee pail down, just outside the fence and Cappy pressed a carefully folded piece of paper into Father Bernard's hand while softly mouthing the word "*ichthys.*"

Father Bernard could hardly believe it and stealthily slid the "precious gift" into his glove. He recalled the stories of the catacombs when it was illegal to be a Christian. To conceal the Eucharist, they referred to it with the Greek word, *ichthys,* which means "fish" because "it is composed of the initial letters of the phrase 'Jesus Christ, Son of God, Savior'."[164] After the meal, in the darkness outside the barrack, the Luxembourgers met a few friends and split the precious host into many small particles placing a small piece on each of their tongues. At that very moment, the Christ Child entered their hearts. They were all giddy with excitement.

***

Toward the end of the week, at midday, a new transport of six-hundred Poles were brought into camp. Most wore summer prison uniforms while some were still dressed in their own clothes. None had caps on their freshly shaven heads, and all were lined up in formation outside in the square shivering in the freezing temperatures. At evening head count, they were still there. Several of the older men, perhaps as many as two dozen, had already collapsed. They were eventually moved into barrack 28, providing the reason why Father Bernard and the others were moved out. They were all who remained of the diocese from which haled the two younger priests who had been arrested earlier. Within six weeks, at least two hundred of them were dead.

***

That Sunday the prisoners were treated to pureed pea soup. Along with the bread ration, it was the most nourishing meal of the entire week. Unfortunately, the head prisoner used the opportunity to inspect the eating utensils, and Father Wampach's mess tin was found to be unacceptable. When the soup was poured, he was passed over. Though Father Bernard was given a full tin, he somehow managed to spill a drop on the floor. Just a drop, but within an instant, the head prisoner was there ripping the tin from Bernard's hands and pouring the contents back into the pail. That night, Wampach and Father Bernard cried at their loss.

January 1942

The first few days of January were extremely cold with temperatures dipping as low as five to fifteen degrees. During those days enormous amounts of snow fell, which made the snow removal detail as painful as it could possibly have been. The prisoners worked from early morning until early evening shoveling, scraping and carting wheelbarrows full of snow, maybe thousands of them, to the brook. The SS and the capos oversaw the operation and were ready with beatings anytime they believed that one of the thousand clergymen slacked off. There was not a moment of rest in the day, and those carting wheelbarrows were required to run. Any pretext of slowing was met with the whack of the SS guard's truncheon. At one point, Father Bernard tripped with his wheelbarrow. It took him a few seconds to get back up, long enough for the SS guard to dash over to him and order him to run with the full load. The SS guard ran beside him and beat him with a leather strap the entire way. Rather than dumping the load of snow in the brook, however, the guard made him run a complete round pushing the same wheelbarrow of snow. When the guard finally left him, Father Bernard tried to remove his hand from the wheelbarrow but was unable to. It had frozen to the handle. He was only able to free himself after blowing on his hand for several minutes. Those who didn't have wheelbarrows were ordered to get tables from the day room, load those tables with snow and carry the loaded tables on their shoulders, in teams of four, to the brook. Each of the men suffered through a day of excruciating pain.

***

In one of the most bizarre episodes of camp life, as if much to this point had been normal, the prisoners were required, with great urgency, to erect a double barrier of tangled barbed wired around barracks 25, 27 and 29. All three barracks were being prepared for the eminent arrival of 300 Russian prisoners of war. The project was so critical that the men were forced to toil day and night. Once completed, the barracks remained empty for three months. When the Russian prisoners finally arrived in March, the three-hundred Russian officers were housed in the barracks for only six weeks before being taken away, never to be seen again. The next day, the clergymen were given three-hundred Russian uniforms and told to disinfect them and then to cut them into strips for the wartime textile collection. No one had to tell the priests that the three-hundred Russian officers had become wartime casualties.

***

Every day at Dachau brought a new experience despite being almost identical to the day prior in so many ways. The daily routine was tired and old, but the pain that resulted from it was fresh and new every day. The suffering was endless, and every chore intensified the pain. There was pain in being dirty but equal or greater pain in showering. There was pain in standing at attention for long hours, but equal pain in reclining in the hard, wooden bunks. There was pain in the monotony of not working, but greater pain from working in the numbing cold with little clothing. There was pain in being beaten, but equal, albeit a different type of pain, in avoiding the beating at the expense of another. Every aspect of life in Dachau caused pain and the suffering was as relentless as the uncertainty of ever having a chance at freedom again. But for Father Bernard, that uncertainty was about to be tested.

Chapter 9

"Ultimately my life, my will, my purpose all comes down to answering these questions:
What is God's plan for my life?
What is God's will for my heart?
What is God's purpose for my life?"

-Father Mike Schmitz
How to Make Great Decisions

The Reprieve
February 1942

February 6, 1942 was the one-year anniversary of his arrest, but Father Bernard was not in a celebratory mood. He had been in Dachau for almost a year and knew better than to indulge in foolish hopes. He was never told the length of his sentence and despite not being hopeful, the thought of his release was in the back of his mind as he stood at attention for the morning head count. "Maybe my sentence is limited," he reasoned. Others had been released after all and some of them had been incarcerated for less than a year. His heart pounded as the camp runner approached his column holding a piece of paper. However, the runner continued on right passed barrack 30 dashing the priest's fleeting hope in an instant.

***

During the morning head count of February 11, however, hope was renewed. The names of his friend, Fathers Schiltz, and another prisoner, Father Michel, were called out. Schiltz walked past Father Bernard with a dazed look on his face and took his place next to the other lucky prisoners in the back of the column. Father Bernard was happy for his friend, but at the same time disappointed that his own name had not been called. He resisted the temptation to look back at Father Schiltz for fear of receiving a beating, and instead focused his attention straight ahead while fighting back the tears of disappointment. During the midday food pail run, Father Bernard did catch a glimpse of Schiltz standing near the kitchen while he waited to depart the camp. Father Bernard waved to him stealthily for fear of getting caught. The gesture spoke volumes of tacit words.

***

Sunday, February 15 was quite an eventful day. First, there was a portion of pea soup at the midday meal. It was the first nutritious meal of a long stretch of otherwise tasteless food and even though he was hunched on the bunk next to Batty, it was wonderful. The glory of the soup almost made him forget that the sky had just begun dropping those insidious snowflakes that piled so deep and caused so much pain to the inmates. The prior weeks had dumped about a foot of snow on the ground, but it was packed down and icy. This fresh coating would need to be shoveled, scraped and carted off.

Father Bernard had barely had a couple of spoons of his soup when the barrack door swung open. "Attention!" an SS guard shouted. "25487! You must come with me immediately!" Someone said, "You're being released."[165] Father Bernard could hardly believe his ears. He handed his soup to Batty and reached instinctively for his hat, coat and clogs, but the SS guard shouted orders to hurry up. Before he could get out the door, Batty stopped him saying, "Comfort my mom."[166]

Bernard glided his way to the administration building staying close to the guard along the way. He needed to remove his clogs to keep up and finally summoned the courage to ask what this was about. The SS guard could offer no definitive explanation other than to speculate that because they were going to see the commandant himself, it must be about a release. Rather than excitement, however, Father Bernard became nervous. "No one is ever released on a Sunday," he reasoned to himself, "and certainly not in the middle of the day."[167]

At the administration building there was no small talk or minced words. After learning that the priest had thirty marks, enough to get to Luxembourg, the commandant told him to be gone in ten minutes, then accompanied him to the facility where prisoners' clothes were stored, a facility which is always closed on Sundays. It all felt like a dream, yet Father Bernard couldn't shake the feeling that something was wrong. The commandant even helped him into his trousers. Something was wrong indeed. He tried to put on his shoes but wasn't able to do so. His feet were terribly swollen as a result of walking barefoot and infected with cuts and chilblains or skin sores and bumps that occur after exposure to very cold temperatures. He did, however, manage to slide into the pair of slippers that he had stored with his clothes. In just over ten minutes, Father Bernard and an SS guard were headed toward the exit gate where Bernard's release papers awaited. He was quickly "handed a form on which [was] printed, *Notification of Release*. The word *Release* ha[d] been crossed out, however, and replaced with [the words] *10 Days' Leave*."[168]

Father Bernard stared at the paper in disbelief. He almost broke down crying when the guard screamed, "Why are you standing around like a total idiot, rev? Go home and bury your mother, stupid!"[169] That was how he learned of his mother's death.

He stood there in disbelief thinking how everything had fallen apart so quickly, until he felt a poke. Not a chastisement with a truncheon, but rather a gentle touch to bring him back to reality. His SS guard said rather sympathetically, "My mother has been dead for a long time...I'm supposed to go to the station with you...but I think you'll be able to find your way by yourself..."[170]

With a blank stare, Father Bernard offered a word of thanks, but he just continued to stand a few feet outside the closed Dachau gate. With his tattered suitcase in one hand, the official leave document in the other, and slippers on his feet, he stood motionless in the snow trying to process the events of the past thirty minutes. It was all too much. As he walked alone to the railroad station, he could think of nothing but his mother; when and how she may have died, whether or not she had already been buried. Then there was the matter of his leave. No one, in the history of Dachau, had ever been granted a leave before. What did it all mean?

The temperature was far below freezing, and the snow was still falling, but Father Bernard had grown accustomed to being cold and the coat layered on top of his shirt, was just something that he couldn't tolerate, so he removed it and draped it across his arm. The walk in the snow was also manageable despite the pain in his feet, and when he reached the town of Dachau, he stopped to ask directions to the railroad station. That is when he took notice of every passerby staring at him. Perhaps it was the cassock and clerical hat, or maybe his gaunt look. He believed he may have even detected a look of pity or empathy.

At the station he learned that the train wouldn't be checking in for an hour, so he used the time to satisfy his ravenous appetite. Despite not having any ration stamps, the owner of the station restaurant noticed his shaved head and loaded him up on massive portions of soup and potatoes. He sat there eating until the train whistle alerted him of its impending departure. In Munich, he had another wait of three hours, so he again journeyed straight to the restaurant. He ate until 2:30 PM, when the restaurant was no longer allowed to serve hot food. The sympathetic waitress handed him some ration stamps and told him to go across the street to the bakery where he was able to get several pieces of cake.

After making a few inquiries, Father Bernard walked to the nearest rectory where the Augustinian priests welcomed him with open arms. There he showered and, once again, was treated to some wonderful food. In addition to generous helpings of all the other food at the table, the priest polished off an entire loaf of bread.

He was feeling much stronger as he headed off to the train station. While waiting to board an express train for Lindau on the Lake of Constance, his mind began to wander. "What if everything I have been told weren't true? Maybe my mother isn't dead at all, and my sisters or some powerful friend have made up the whole story in order to offer me an opportunity to escape?"[171] He was again filled with hope and thought about how he might stay at some rectory in Lindau for a few days before escaping under the cover of darkness to Switzerland in a rowboat or perhaps swimming with a life jacket!...The thoughts were fleeting though and he crashed to reality knowing that his mother's death must have been verified before his leave was granted. Further, the concept of a leave was so extraordinary, that someone must have had to guarantee his return. He boarded the train and headed for home. It was a long trip, but the priest's mind was devoid of any thoughts as exhaustion set in. As soon as he arrived home and hugged his brothers and sisters, he began to cry... like a baby.

He visited the cemetery to offer his last goodbye to the woman who gave him life and so much more. Then he reported to Gestapo headquarters at the Villa Pauly, which was required as a condition of his temporary release. There, during a discussion with Friedrich, the Secretary of the Criminal Police, he learned the possible reason for his release though it was certainly not relayed to him, but rather, inferred by him. After making small talk by inquiring about his stay at Dachau and the stay of his fellow Luxembourg clergymen, Friedrich got right to the point. Have they had enough? Don't they want to come home? That's when it hit Father Bernard like a ton of bricks. "It would be a great propaganda success: Six Luxembourg clergymen return home after being 're-educated' at Dachau."[172] For a moment, he thought about the extraordinary responsibility being thrust upon him. He, through his answers, may well have been responsible for the lives of his friends. But before he could dwell on the possibilities, Friedrich continued. "Well, how is it?" "Have the gentlemen's attitudes softened up a bit in the meantime?"[173] Father Bernard visualized his friends, freezing, starving and otherwise miserable. He looked at Friedrich and thought for a moment. "At the same time...a face appears before me, as if carved in stone, teeth gritted, with an ambivalent expression, revealing both unspeakable suffering and at the same time an infinite, almost mocking contempt. This was the mask that Batty Esch wore every day at camp." 'You'll have to ask them yourself,'"[174] Bernard responded.

Friedrich must have acknowledged the defeat he had just been handed. He sat in silence for a moment then told Father Bernard that he would likely be released soon. Even if he had to go back for a while, it wouldn't be for long. For the priest, the thought of imminent release was a chain that kept him firmly bound more than even a guard post in front of his family home could have. Having complied with the order to visit Gestapo headquarters, Father Bernard rose from his chair to depart. As he did, Friedrich reminded him that he had a big family. Bernard recognized the statement as the threat it was intended to be. The next day, he celebrated Holy Mass for the first time in ten months. The remainder of the leave was uneventful and passed rather quickly.

Part IV

Chapter 10

"No one should want to be united on the path to perdition."

Return To Camp

On February 25, 1942, Father Bernard boarded his train for the return trip to Dachau. He thought briefly about his chance to free himself and his compatriots, but knew that he would not have been able to live with himself, regardless of how free and well fed he and his friends were, if his actions might have helped lead to a Nazi victory in the war or even misleading some into thinking the Third Reich was virtuous in any way. He simply refused to be used as a pawn in the Nazi power grab and the ethnic cleansing to which the regime endeavored. Instead, he focused his attention on the misery of Dachau vowing to undergo the pain and torture, as Jesus did, for the right reasons. It was time to readjust his mental attitude and return to survival mode. It was perhaps beneficial to his psyche that he did not yet realize that "the real hell was only about to begin."[175]

He ate three hardboiled eggs on the return trip and was standing at the Dachau gate at 5:00 PM on the dot, just as was required of him. The man at the gate could not believe what he was seeing. He stared at the priest, mouth agape, for a few minutes before going to get instructions. Then, with relative haste, the priest was processed back into camp.

While exchanging his civilian clothes for a new prison uniform, one that would have to be altered to fit better, he waved a ham sandwich and a pack of Dutch cigarillos at the SS guard. The man recognized the bribe instinctively and took the cigarillos while allowing the priest to keep the ham sandwich, which Father Bernard gave to Batty upon his arrival back to barrack 30. His friends, who thought he had been released permanently, were all stunned to see him back at camp. He dreaded the return, but at least he was assigned to room one again with Batty, who had already retreated to a corner to wolf down the sandwich.

Later in the evening, the prisoners gathered in the street outside the barrack and Father Bernard told them all about home, the war, the resistance, and about all the far-fetched hopes, anything that might give them hope and provide some comfort. For their part, the others shared information with Father Bernard. They told him that Representative Wayrich died in camp during a lung operation and that Franz Clement suffered from extreme eczema that covered his entire head. Father Wampach was relocated to room 4 with Father Stoffels. Finally, starting in March, any prisoner not already assigned work would be required to work in the "plantation."

The plantation was an extremely large cultivated area of former marsh land that was used primarily to grow medicinal plants. Its conversion from a marsh area to a "farm" had cost hundreds if not thousands of human lives. It had several paths running through it, and a work obligation there was one of the most feared assignments imaginable. Work in the plantation didn't really count as labor and therefore carried no extra ration of food. It was simply a way to utilize prisoners who were unfit for any other work. Yet the work was grueling. Regardless of weather conditions, the prisoners were required to work on their knees, pulling weeds and crawling through ditches filled with foul-smelling, motionless water. There was no hope of finding shelter from the elements. Workers were exposed to wind, rain and the capos who treated them like cattle. Every prisoner did all in his power to avoid that work detail. Even Batty's transport commando was preferable and those workers received an extra ration. Batty promised that he would try to get Father Bernard an assignment in transport commando number 3 with him.

***

To the guards' delight, the last few days of February were among the snowiest on record, and the prisoners were required to shovel, scrape and transport until some literally worked themselves into unconsciousness. The commandant watched with glee through his window above the entryway. The capos were urged to maintain the prisoners' tempo even if beatings were required to keep them moving. Wheelbarrow after wheelbarrow, and table after table, were pushed and carried by the prisoners to the point of near death. When the whistle signaling that it was time to go carry the food pails finally blew, the men were actually relieved.

March 1942

Wednesday, March 18, 1842 started out to be excessively grueling. Father Bernard was required to carry his pail a long distance and, as one of the last men to return to the barrack, was already exhausted. Just as he reached the door, the camp capo pushed past him and ordered seventeen men to fall in immediately. Certain that it would mean work outside the camp, Father Bernard returned outside and stood in formation. The line marched to the labor office and stood at attention while the men were inspected for worthiness. He tried to stand upright so his fatigue wouldn't show. Thankfully, he was one of the sixteen who passed inspection and were told that they would from that point be known as the Transport Commando Praezifix. That phrase was most unsettling for Father Bernard. Through camp experience he knew that Praezifix was another one of the hardest work assignments at camp. He took solace, however, in knowing that he would receive an extra ration.

The men were issued authentic shoes with thick wooden soles, warmer coats, gloves, and better caps. They were introduced to their capo and told to report to their wagon the next morning following the head count.

The thought of being removed from the constant torment of the head prisoner in the barrack was so exciting that Father Bernard could hardly sleep that night. He would no longer be present during locker inspections. Nor would he be required to shovel snow, deliver wheelbarrows of coal or carry food pails. The midday meal would be eaten outside of the camp confines. He would be able to see some of the places outside of Dachau and, above all, there would be plenty to eat.

At 5:30 AM the men lined up for head count. It was March 19, the feast day of Saint Joseph the Worker. The cart to which he was assigned was identical to the one Batty pulled with all the same manpower positions. As soon as the tally was completed, the group of seventeen ran to the wagon, hitched up, and galloped off toward the front of the camp where they received their work assignment. They were also assigned three armed SS guards, and soon the entire contingent disappeared through the front gates. The cart was empty except for a box of bread for which all the prisoners longed.

The capo explained that the primary task of Transport Commando Praezifix was to deliver the soup pails from the camp kitchen to the various external work crews who eat their midday meal outside the camp walls and to return the empty pails back to the kitchen. In between, they were required to do whatever work the Dachau Praezifix factory might assign. The factory manufactured screws, and aside from some factory clean-up, the crew was required to transport machines and material from the old Dachau factory, to the new factory under construction outside the town limits.

Father Bernard's position on the wagon was on the right side, pulling on the same cable as Stani Suske, a young Polish priest from Warsaw. The two happened to be about the same height and strength, a critical factor when two people are harnessed together. And, because Suske spoke a little French, the two priests were able to carry on a conversation right in front of the capo and guards.

It was fairly easy to pull the wagon along a level road, but it didn't take long for the prisoners' feet to begin to ache. Their feet were still swollen, and the priests were not accustomed to wearing such stiff, heavy shoes. Before nighttime, all the skin on the prisoner's feet was rubbed raw. Even that condition, however, was less painful than having to curl their toes on each step when wearing the clogs. Making the trek a bit worse was the snow. Though it had thawed in the middle of the road, the prisoners pulling from the side of the wagon were forced to wade through melting snow and water that accumulated along the sides of the road.

It took only about twenty minutes to reach the first row of houses in the town of Dachau, but that is where the wagon had to turn off the road and follow along a small path between the gardens. While off road, the team had to gallop faster to prevent from getting stuck in the mud and snow. The real danger, though, was of getting crushed between the lurching wagon and the wall. It was about 7:00 AM when they reach their destination at Praezifix, rolling the wagon through the open gate and into the expansive yard of the factory.

Father Bernard and two others were ordered into the factory. There, between the many lathes, they collected and carried out iron shavings. Though there was a broom standing only feet away, the men collected the shavings off the floor with their bare hands, being careful not to get splinters from the incredibly sharp shards. Those remaining outside were told to shovel coal and clean up. Suske managed to pull the best job assignment. He was placed in charge of the central heating in the Chief's villa. As such, he was able to sit in a dry, warm room with no supervision whatsoever.

After working for less than an hour, the whistle sounded, alerting the priests that it was time to assemble once again. This time they had to transport two cigar-box-sized cardboard boxes full of screws, to the train station. It made no sense to anyone why they would need eighteen prisoners, a wagon, three guards and a five-ton trailer to carry these two very small boxes, but what the prisoners didn't know was the first law of all external work details; no one on the detail was allowed to split off from the others for any reason. So, the prisoners pulled the heavy wagon through the muddy path, along the road, and to the train station, and then back again. Father Bernard learned that day that it just doesn't pay to think logically about anything that happens at Dachau.

At 9:30 AM the inmates on Transport Commando Praezifix were given a break and their extra ration. A generous portion of bread, carefully prepared and counted, was distributed to each priest. They were also given a piece of liverwurst. The capo informed the men that twice a week they would also be allowed margarine on the bread. The priests took a seat on a pile of coal and savored the moment. Father Bernard could recall nothing at Dachau ever tasting so good. He felt totally transformed after consuming the feast; like he could suddenly accomplish anything. That feeling quickly abated, however, when about an hour later they were again hitched to the wagon headed for camp.

At Dachau they went straight for the kitchen where the men loaded the wagon with the soup pails for all six external work crews. The soup of the day was turnip, but there were twenty-five quarts for only eighteen men. Bernard was overjoyed at the abundance of the day's meal.

Transporting the lunch pails, brimming with soup, to the worksites over bumpy roads and paths, without spilling any would be no small feat, but the men knew that spillage would result in certain beatings by the SS. Despite the heavy load, the travel back to New Praezifix was successful and, without a beating, the priest crew enjoyed their own midday meal while sitting in some type of shed. There was enough soup to allow each man as much as three pints. Though the soup was mostly water, it did fill them up. Of course, the SS guards had their own food, which was far better than that of the inmates. Whatever was left over from the guard's meal was given to the capo, which in turn compensated him for the risky nature of his job.

As soon as the meal had been completed, an order arrived by telephone to pick up a load of sand from a gravel pit at the Old Praezifix factory building. The work was arduous because the men, who were standing in a gravel pit, were required to toss each shovel full of sand a significant distance to reach the wagon. One of the men broke down crying, saying, "It's impossible, we're not up to anything anymore. It's too late for us." Father Bernard ignored the man's words and, in a rage of frustration, shoveled even faster.

With the full cart, the men worked the wagon to the factory site and unloaded its contents. After a stretch of less strenuous work inside the factory, the men set out for camp. It was about 5:00 PM. On the way they retrieved the empty pails from the six work crews and galloped back into camp where all the other prisoners had been standing at attention waiting for the evening head count.

Following the count, the capo took the Transport Commando Praezifix team to the infirmary to have their feet bandaged. The socks were stuck to open wounds with dried blood, and when finally extracted, their feet look like raw meat. One crew member flinched when the infirmary attendant ripped the sock off his foot. He was roundly disciplined with a slap to the ear. Then the capo reminded everyone that he can use only healthy men for the work assignment, and they will have to get used to jogging up to eighteen kilometers, or more than eleven miles per day in those stiff, heavy shoes.

***

Every day was pretty much the same on Transport Commando Praezifix. The team grew closer and the running became a bit easier as they became more accustomed to the distance. The capo turned out to be a bit more compassionate than other capos at the camp. Father Bernard witnessed that consideration firsthand when a man collapsed from exhaustion. Rather than a beating, he was laid on the wagon until he was able to resume work. In addition, the weakest or sickliest men were placed at the back of the wagon hitch where it was easier to slack off without being noticed by the guards.

On about the fourth day, the crew ran into trouble as soon as they pulled the wagon into the Praezifix factory yard. It appeared that the furnace man allowed the heat to go out twice the previous night at the chief engineer's private quarters. Stani Suske, whose job it was to maintain the furnace, anticipated a severe beating, but instead, was told he was being replaced on the job. "Who can do a better job?"[176] the chief engineer yelled. When no one volunteered, Father Bernard, hoping not to upset the factory owner, stepped forward.

His new domain was a paradise. The work was in the private villa, and there was no guard standing over him. While there were people upstairs in the house, Father Bernard worked alone in the basement. The solitude felt amazing to someone who heretofore had to perform even the most private bodily functions amidst a vast audience. The basement consisted of four walls, a huge furnace and a pile of coal. There was also a stack of firewood and a wooden block that was the most comfortable seat in the house. He basked in the warmth of the furnace for several minutes.

There was a stack of potatoes that the furnace man was not allowed to touch under penalty of death, but hunger has a way of instilling a criminal element in even the most honest man. He selected a few of the finest spuds from the pile and tucked them under the ashes. A couple of times he went up to the yard to be sure the house didn't smell of roasted potatoes, and then settled down to the finest meal of all his days in camp.

His work routine included splitting wood for kindling down to matchstick size, piling the kindling into a crate, and feeding the crate load through the furnace door. This process was repeated several times throughout the day. He also shoveled coal from one corner to another and back again. He swept the floor and dusted things off. His primary function, it might be said, was to look busy in the event that someone entered the basement.

One of the brighter moments for Father Bernard came when a young child, Methilde, would talk to him through the crack in the door. He never saw her, as the girl sat on the upper step of the staircase which bent around a corner, but the girl's innocent voice alone was "like a ray of light from heaven for [him]."[177] He told her wonderful stories and "rediscovered [his] faith in beauty and purity, in innocence and love."[178] Because he never saw her face, Father Bernard's image of her was as wild as his imagination. It was the best therapy God could have afforded him. It wasn't all pleasurable, however. Frequently, there was more demanding work outside and Father Bernard was required to help support the team. He found those days were particularly hard after the little taste of heaven in the basement.

On one day, after a particularly exhausting morning of delivering cement to the New Praezifix, one of the men opened the lid of the soup pail just a few seconds before the whistle blew. The SS guard just happened to see the whole incident and was not about to let it go unpunished. He pushed the prisoner out of the way and tipped the pail over. The men watched as their entire lunch soaked into the sand. Instead of eating the men were ordered to march. As each man walked by the SS guard who stood at the door, he was hit on the head with a large board.

Back at camp, Father Bernard learned that Batty Esch was in declining health and growing very weak. From that point, Bernard consumed only his soup each day, saving the bread for Batty in the evenings. Father Wampach, who had been assigned to cleaning the SS men's barracks, also came across something edible while emptying the garbage pails. He was providing some extra food to Stoffels and Brachmond, who were also suffering from malnutrition. The men were still required to report for work detail, regardless of their physical condition, and this was certainly not helping their recovery.

In an effort to help them, Father Bernard decided to attempt the near impossible. He tried to smuggle two potatoes from the stores in the basement of the villa in which he worked. Stuffing one into each pocket, he arrived at camp, late as they usually were, only to find that the guards were conducting an inspection by frisking each man upon reentry to the camp. He thought of tossing the potatoes under the wagon but was being too closely watched to take the risk. He knew that getting caught would result in a severe beating if not death but saw no way out at that point. The SS platoon leader stepped toward the men and shouted, "Turn out your pockets!" Just then, the camp commandant arrived for the head count of the prisoners in camp who were already lined up at attention. "Dismissed," the SS leader yelled. Father Bernard breathed a sigh of relief and ran to his mates who were already standing in line.

***

Punishment, it seemed, just could not be avoided, however. On the following Sunday morning both Bernard and Batty were disciplined for poor bed-making activities. They were sentenced to work in the gold mine, a euphemism for the bathroom. Here, prisoners were assigned the task of collecting the contents of the latrine into buckets and subsequently emptying the full buckets on the grass of the yard in front of the barrack. The buckets had no handles, though, and the contents would frequently spill over onto the prisoner as he jogged out to the yard. Considering all the other forms of punishment this really wasn't too bad.

The end of March brought additional snow, which the priests, regardless of other work assignments, still had to shovel, scrape and cart away. If that wasn't bad enough, a new capo assigned to Transport Commando Praezifix was as much of a monster as had been known to the camp. His goal was to destroy the wagon, knowing that there was no replacement, thereby putting an end to that work detail. This was his objective because he liked neither the detail nor the amount of running it entailed and hoped to land a better job for himself once the Praezifix transport was terminated. To achieve his objective, he ordered the men to load the wagons so full that the wheels wobbled, until, one day, one of the wheels shattered under the weight. The "accident" ended the Transport Commando Praezifix. For Father Bernard it meant far more than the loss of a work assignment. It represented the end of double-ration soup, work in a warm and comfortable cellar of the chief engineer's villa, and the indulgence of roasted potatoes. The new assignment offered no such perks.

Holy Week
March 30 Through April 5, 1942

The first week of April found Father Bernard without an assignment and once again crammed in the barrack, suffering from hunger, vulnerable to abuse and harassment, and forced to perform exercises all day. It turned out to be one of the worse weeks of his camp experience.

April 3 was Good Friday and the entire morning was spent standing at attention in the assembly yard in the pouring rain. At midday, they marched to the kitchen to fetch soup pails. Exhausted and hungry, the prisoners of barrack 30 returned to quarters, only to find the entire contents of the barrack; tables, stools, straw mattresses, the contents of all the lockers, including bread, towels and bowls, tossed on the rain-soaked street. The barrack windows and doors were also open. Standing there in disbelief, the priests heard the order,

> "Fall in! One of you bastards was hiding foreign currency, and it was found! As punishment, everything in blocks 28 and 30 will be thrown outside twice a day for the next week. Twice a day you will put it back in perfect order, everything cleaned off, and the beds remade. You will dust and sweep until not one piece of straw is visible on the street. There will be no food until evening, and then only after the clerk has made a personal inspection."[179]

This was how the priests had to spend their midday and end-of-day breaks for the next seven days. The prisoners were horrified. They knew there was simply no way that a prisoner, subjected to the hazing that new arrivals are put through, could ever smuggle foreign money into the camp. Furthermore, even if one could get the forbidden currency past the orientation process, it would serve no purpose for a prisoner to have foreign money. It was of no use to them. The priests knew the accusation was a pretext and believed that they knew why. The Vatican radio station had broadcast a report critical of the treatment of priests at Dachau. For that radio protest, the priests had to be punished.

After order was restored to the barrack, the prisoners were required to exercise: to run, do up-and-down exercises and deep knee bends for the entire afternoon. After returning from the dinner pail run, they had to do it all over again. Only after everything was clean were they allowed to eat dinner. When they finished eating, they all collapsed into bed, the bed they had just spent so much time making up with precision.

Day after day, the prisoners of the working barrack would toss everything out of barracks 28 and 30, stealing whatever they could in the process, and each time the prisoners of barracks 28 and 30 would restore the order, clean everything up and exercise. By the end of the week, between seventy and eighty priests were dead and the remaining fifteen hundred were sapped of all their energy.

April 7 Through April 30, 1942

On April 7, the Tuesday following Easter, work detail resumed for the former Praezifix Commando seventeen. The new assignment required persons to very quickly prepare a meadow for planting. That's when the men realized just how much of a toll the past week had taken on them. No extra ration was allowed because the work wasn't considered by the SS guards to be serious labor. Only the capo was provided extra bread.

Father Bernard was the only non-Polish priest on the detail, so the capo would sometimes talk to him, generally about religious matters. These discussions were most welcomed as they provided the priest short respites during the day. Sometimes the SS guard would join in. Father Bernard would talk about the free will God has given us and how revealing Himself to us too clearly would essentially force us to believe thereby taking away our free will. The discussions were cordial but always ended with the SS guards saying, "It's all nonsense and lies! And now get back to work!"[180] The talks ended abruptly however when the capo exclaimed that despite all the talk, he still didn't believe in God. Father Bernard unwisely responded, "then why do you talk about Him so much?" There were no more theological discussions after that.

On April 19, the work order was revised. The meadow was only about thirty percent dug when all the priests of Dachau were ordered to work on the plantation. Like work in the meadow, this work was also considered "too light" to qualify for the extra rations. The following morning, fifteen-hundred non-German clergymen were marched to the south gate. The work detail was actually off the plantation and the men were required to transform a square tract of marshland into an agricultural field. The overseer of the project was the most feared capo in Dachau, a man by the name of Rasch. Many of the priests did not survive this detail.

Upon arrival at 6:30 AM, the priests were divided into groups of thirty men, each with its own capo. Each group was assigned equipment. Some were given very heavy wheelbarrows, some were provided rollers, and still others, shovels and spades. Father Bernard's commando was forced to carry gravel to the furthest end of the path where twelve men were pushing a roller over the gravel after it was dumped. Because of the uneven terrain, many of the wheelbarrows broke under the weight of the load.

At 9:30 AM, two prisoners walked onto the worksite carrying a large basket. They walk up to the priest and then right past them laughing as they gave the extra ration of bread and sausage to the capo. By Noon, Father Bernard was so exhausted and weak that he didn't think he would survive the day. When the flag was finally waved signifying the midday break, the priests were told to jog to the far end of the field and join the others who were waiting to march back to camp.

They were not granted a lot of time to eat. In groups of one hundred, the priests were required to wash their shoes in one of the five basins until they were spotless. Upon completion they were ordered to sit at the table quietly until all had completed the chore. Only then was the lid lifted from the soup enabling them to eat. They finished their soup quickly and immediately began sweeping and cleaning the room until it was time for the midday head count.

The afternoon work detail was much easier than that of the morning session. In the second half of the day the priests only had to carry buckets of loam to the field to fertilize the marshy soil.

They moved in single file, filling the buckets from the truck and emptying them onto the field. To avoid punishment, they tried to keep out of view of capo Rasch, but were able to avoid his gaze only for as long as the line kept moving. Occasionally, the prisoners were even able to pretend to fill the bucket, catching a nice breather on the return trip to the marsh.

There were some perks to working the marsh. There were edible plants, such as dandelions, that grew there. A Czech priest offered Father Bernard a root resembling a finger, telling him that it contained fat. Father Bernard took and devoured it. It turned out not to be such a good thing, however. The root had no taste but simply coated his tongue with a slick layer of fat. Ultimately, it made him dreadfully sick. He never ate another one.

The best growth, however, was found near the compost pile, and the prisoners loved when their work brought them close to that location. There were much tastier plants there including the little green peas that were planted a few days earlier and had just started to sprout. Rhubarb, another delicacy growing near the compost heap, must have grown from seeds that fell in the prior year. And tender red cabbage leaves could also be found there.

If one were to hesitate even for a second, the opportunity to grab a plant would pass him by. The prisoner had to be both quick and stealth if he had any hope of snagging one of nature's extra bounties. That is exactly how Father Bernard managed to get some delicacies one particular day. He had eyed a certain patch of dandelions for a few days but had no opportunity to grab them. At night he would relive the moment he passed by them thinking of ways to make some his, promising himself that he would make an extra meal out of them. On one April day, as the prisoners marched in single file toward the site, he spotted them just ahead. As he approached, he tossed his cap into the thick patch of yellow flowers. He quickly stepped out of line to fetch it, lifting some dandelions up with the cap. Both the cap and the flowers went onto his head. That day, he enjoyed the bounty.

At other times being sneaky didn't pay off. Such was the case when Batty snagged some powder from the kitchen. He proudly took Father Bernard's hand and put it in his pocket saying, "I've stolen something." It felt like a pulverized substance, and Father Bernard asked what it was. "That is soup powder. It's a mixture of different vegetables that have been dried and finely ground," Batty said. "There's a whole sack full of it at the plantation storage room. I bet it will be good in our soup. The bishop took some too."[181]

The latter comment may have allayed some of the priests' concerns about the theft. Each of them dropped a healthy portion into their soup. "The stuff began to rise like cake batter, the whole soup turned thick and stiff and took on such a fiery hot taste that after the first spoonful [they] had to rush out to cool [their] burning mouths at the water faucet. The soup was inedible."[182]

The prisoners had to be very careful about bending down to take one of these morsels from the plantation ground, Being caught eating from the field was considered theft and sabotage. Such crimes would prompt a beating at best or an appointment with the firing squad at worst. On one particularly cold and windy day, the work crew for which Batty Esch and Brachmond worked was frisked before the midday meal and bits of green dust, traces of their theft from the morning prior, had been found in their pockets. They were stripped naked and forced to kneel facing a wall for the balance of the day while SS guards poured buckets of cold water on them. The two men returned to camp that evening "more dead than alive."[183] In addition, the two priests lost their plush work assignment on the drying room crew, and the next day were assigned to Father Bernard's commando. Fortunately, they managed, however, to escape the threatened punishment of twenty-five lashes with a horsewhip or two hours hanging on the tree because no report was filed by the capo, thanks to some smooth talking by Brachmond.

There was no real boundary around the marsh. One had to imagine an invisible line connecting guard posts to ensure that he remained inside the work area. One priest stepped outside the area to relieve himself. Immediately there was the sound of rifle fire from the guard post. It may have been only a warning, but the unharmed priest quickly rejoined the others, albeit looking a bit more ghostly than he had looked just moments prior. Once back in the line, he was roundly and viciously beaten by the capo.

***

Each day brought more prisoners to Dachau, and Luxembourgers were still arriving to camp on a regular basis. The most recent arrivals included Father Dupong and Professor Emil Schaus. Through the barbed-wire fence, Father Bernard was able to trade greetings with his good friends who were being housed in newcomers block 9. Father Bernard always had mixed emotions about being reunited with good friends at Dachau. He enjoyed seeing them and their presence brought such consolation, but he detested the fact that they were caught up in arrests and would now be subjected to the daily torture that was camp life.

***

The weather turned particularly nasty during the early weeks of spring. It was cold, extremely windy and it rained constantly. The work crews had no overcoats for a long time and were often soaked to the skin by the time they arrived in the work area. When they finally were issued coats, the capo used them as a means of inflicting punishments, often making the priests remove their jackets for the slightest infraction and forcing them to work in their shirtsleeves. That was the punishment for the entire crew when one priest was found to have done something as small as turning up his collar.

While in camp, at least for the time that Batty and Fr. Bernard worked together, they would spend the early morning praying, confessing to one another, each giving the other absolution. "That provided a significant comfort to [them]. [They] felt calmer, more serene, and that did [them] good physically."[184]

May Through July 1942

The prisoners arrived back to camp for the midday meal one day in early May but were not allowed entry. While waiting in the afternoon sun, several thoughts flooded the minds of the work crew and speculation spread in whispers. Are we being frisked? Was someone caught with contraband? All the speculation was wrong, however. The actual reason for the delayed entrance was that there were visitors on the campus. The routine was always the same when the camp was being inspected by visitors. The external work crews were denied entry while the other inmates were forced to disappear into the barracks and remain out of view. Only a select number of well-nourished capos were allowed to be seen by any visitors and they were required to walk "up and down the camp street between the lawn and the decorative saplings...looking contented."[185]

Visitors were always allowed into the same places in the camp. The changing room and showers, the highly polished kitchen where the visitors could view their own reflections in the tile floor and in the cooking vat. They were also taken to the laundry facility, the disinfection site, and the clothes storage facilities, and the infirmary, which was equipped with the last word in modern medical technology. Finally, they were taken to a single barrack, barrack 2, which had been converted into a showplace. The floors were always waxed to a high shine and the beds made up with fine linen. Everything about it was warm and comfortable, right down to the six prisoners, honor inmates, really. Their heads were full of coiffured hair, and they looked healthy and fit. It was their camp job to be sure that the premises were ready at any time for an inspection. The other inmates, the visitors were always told, were "outside working at the moment." In reality, however, they were "standing outside the gate, shivering from hunger and fatigue, following the visitors through camp in their imaginations and wondering anxiously if there will be enough time left to eat their midday soup."[186] Several of the men waiting at the gate collapsed and were later taken to the infirmary. They were never seen again.

The gates were finally opened enabling the prison work crew to enter the camp. Almost as soon as they had started marching inside, however, a camp runner approached yelling for them to get back outside. The visitors were still in camp, and the prisoners had to remain unseen. The work team scattered in all directions, even without instruction from the capo, diving for cover behind the far ends of the barracks. When the visitors actually departed, the priests were granted an extra thirty minutes to eat their soup. It was a reward for their cooperation.

**

On May 28, Father Stoffels arrived unexpectedly from the infirmary accompanied by a capo. "I've been assigned to a transport,"[187] he said. Father Wampach gathered together Stoffels' few possessions. Father Bernard and the others knew that he would be killed that day, but Father Stoffels told them not to look so sad, "We're simply going to another camp....It's supposed to be much better there."[188] Father Stoffels just didn't understand the level of malice that existed among the men of the SS. Nor did he suspect anything would occur other than a transfer. Father Wampach spoke to him alone for a few moments, probably giving him final absolution. Then, kissing Fathers Wampach, Esch, Brachmond, and Bernard, Father Stoffels marched off. Father Bernard reasoned that Father Sotffels would indeed be far better off in the other camp. Then he wept.

The capos were intent on destroying what remained of morale among the priests and, on a regular basis, did what they could to deliver either physical or psychological pain, all adding to the priest's fatigue. On this day, however, the clergymen were able to turn the tables a bit.

"The priests are going to be assigned to the crematorium commando," the head prisoner of barrack 30 told the barrack clerk just loud enough for the priests to hear. If he was certain that this work assignment would punish the clergymen, he was surely disappointed to hear some of the priests' comments. "Then from now on the dead will be buried in the presence of a priest," and "At the very least we can secretly say the prayers for the dead."[189] After overhearing those remarks, the capos decided against assigning the priests to the crematorium commando.

The captive priests were growing weaker by the day. And by the time Pentecost Sunday arrived on June 1, the extreme hunger had turned to starvation. Their weakened condition didn't stop the SS from inflicting more torture on them, however. Thirty men were selected from each room of the priests' barracks. Father Bernard was among the men selected from room one. They marched to an open space in front of the disinfection building to an enormous pile of clothing. The uniforms, which were cut into narrow strips, were instantly recognizable as those belonging to the Russian men who had long since disappeared from camp. The priests were instructed to sort the strips by color with the threat of being denied food until the task was complete. They started in immediately hoping that the job might be completed in time for at least one meal. Some men became dizzy and faint. One vomited into the pile, but all kept working until it was time for the evening headcount. The job had not been finished, and that meant that, in addition to missing the midday meal, there would be no dinner for the priests either.

The next day, a transport commando team raked and shoveled all the sorted strips back into a single pile, loaded them into a wagon and hauled them away. Batty Esch was feeling the effects of hunger more than Father Bernard, who believed his friend was in his last days. Father Bernard raced from prisoner to prisoner begging for anything that might provide Batty with a little sustenance. He found a small gold mine of food and quickly brought it to Batty who wept at the site of it. Eating the extra meal, however, didn't ease his despair and he still exhibited a "what's the use" mentality.

***

Unable to work through the entire day on the plantation with only the midday meal break, it became necessary for the prisoners to find some alternative method of resting. They found it in the plantation's latrine. Originally, the latrine was a hastily constructed horizontal pole mounted on two posts securely driven into the ground. The pole was about eighteen inches high and could accommodate up to four men. Later, it was improved with privacy curtains made from old sacks. The curtain was not so much for privacy between the priests, as all pretense of modesty had long since been lost. It was more for providing a space outside the view of the capos, thereby enabling the prisoner to sneak in a much-needed rest. A ten-minute walk to the latrine, a ten-minute stay, including waiting time, and a ten-minute walk back to the work site, allowed for a thirty-minute work break. Consequently, it became a meeting place for prisoners from various exterior work commandos. As an added benefit, the latrine was located next to a very large compost pile where, on occasion, an edible morsel could be found. Even leftovers from the SS dogs would sometimes have enough meat remaining on the bone to provide a much-needed source of protein for the starving captives. The capos frowned on any scavenging by prisoners, however, and would beat them if they were caught.

There was a particular day when a capo was discarding a basket full of discarded leek seedlings at the compost site as a group of men in line for the latrine looked on. He scattered the contents of the basket on the compost heap and then, while looking directly at the prisoners, urinated on the seedlings, adding, "That's so you'll lose your appetites."[190] The little act of grotesqueness did not dissuade some of the hungrier men. As soon as the coast was clear, they gathered up the seedlings and consumed them as if they came right from the market.

***

Father Bernard was so exhausted that he entertained the thought of intentionally collapsing hoping to be taken to the infirmary where he might rest for a few hours, but seeing how fallen prisoners were treated, he, heeding the sound advice from Father Nick Wampach, thought better of doing it.

As work continued seemingly without end, Batty Esch whispered, "That's number five today." Father Bernard looked around to see to what Esch was referring when he noticed a body lying face down in the mud. Apparently, Father Stani Suske could bear no more and had collapsed that day. A few priests dragged him out of the muddy puddle and left him next to the work equipment. The others continued to pull the tiny weeds from the very long dike that the prisoners constructed from dirt on previous days. Father Suske lay next to the equipment until the end of the workday, at which point he was taken to the infirmary. The speculation was that he'd never be seen or heard from again.

Father Bernard thought for days about what Father Wampach had told him about feigning collapse. He knew the risks involved and weighed them against the potential benefit. It might be difficult to accomplish but pretending to collapse and being taken to the infirmary for a recovery period was the only way he figured that he might continue to make it. In his mind, the alternative was dying in the fields from exhaustion. He devised a plan and waited until an optimum time to implement it.

Then, following another particularly gruesome day in the field, he realized that the time had come. Even if not optimum, his poor physical condition would prevent him from going on too much longer. Plus, the clergymen were behind schedule at the end of the workday, and that was in his favor. It meant that the capo or SS would not have a lot of time to devote to him when he collapsed. So, on the jog back to camp Father Bernard whispered to Batty, who happened to be jogging next to him, alerting him to the plan. Then he went down hard hitting his face on the asphalt. He was now in full acting mode, though it didn't take an Oscar-winning performance to feign exhaustion. The men behind him, also dead tired, tumbled on top of Father Bernard. From his position on the ground, Father Bernard heard curses and then felt a couple of sharp blows to the ribs, which helped roll him over. Seeing his weakened and bloodied condition, the capo ordered some others to load him into a wheelbarrow and told Batty to trundle him back to camp. Batty engaged in a slow run. That was all he could manage in his own weakened condition.

As Batty maneuvered the wheelbarrow, Father Bernard's head, which was hanging backward over the front edge, was scraping against the wheel. It was tearing piece after piece of his scalp off, but there was little he could do about it. Batty unloaded the wheelbarrow contents in time for head count, which took about an hour. Of course, Father Bernard was not required to stand at attention as the other men were. He took full advantage of the episode to lie down. After head count, he and the other priests who reported ill were checked by the SS doctor. Most of them were returned to duty with kicks and punches. Father Bernard prayed to his guardian angel as he waited for his turn to be examined. When his turn came, the doctor ordered him to the infirmary.

The Infirmary

After checking into the medical unit, Father Bernard had to relinquish his prison garb in exchange for a fresh shirt and a wool blanket, then he was ordered to lie down. The room held more than one-hundred prisoners and was completely full, in many cases with two and three men sharing a straw sack. As he hunted for a place to lie down, he was met with glares from the others who were afraid that he might invade some of their space. Before he could locate a spot, he felt a tug on his shirt followed by an invitation from a professor at a Polish seminary to lie next to him.

Father Bernard had not felt more relaxed in months. He was stretched out and quietly laying down with no worries about work, head counts, cleaning rooms, making beds, fetching soup pails – nothing but quiet relaxation. He closed his eyes and wondered "if it could be any better in heaven."[191]

The meal that evening was barley soup, and Father Bernard told his bed mate, who was unable to sit up, of its arrival. "Do we get the same ration as outside,"[192] he inquired of him, but he got no reply. When he turned to ask the professor again, he discovered that the man was dead. Father Bernard tilted the seminarian's head toward him and quietly performed his priestly office while thinking that he had become acquainted with a saint. Then, quietly turning the dead man's head in the other direction so the capo wouldn't notice he had died, Father Bernard enjoyed both his and the professor's rations of soup.

Only after the meal did Father Bernard let someone know that the professor was dead. The prisoner serving as the infirmary attendant didn't listen for a heartbeat or check for a pulse. He didn't even hold a mirror to his nose to check for a breath. He instead opened the man's mouth and yelled to the clerk, "Two," referencing the number of gold teeth that the dead man had. Then his shirt was cut off, and he was dragged naked across the floor to the washroom where he was covered with a blanket. His body remained in the washroom until morning when he was taken to the crematorium. For Father Bernard, the good man's misfortune meant that he now had the straw sack all to himself.

The bunk placement didn't last too long, however, as the following morning Father Bernard was told to climb to the top bunk. The lower bunks, he was told, were for those too weak to climb. It took every ounce of energy for Father Bernard to make the ascent, but he managed, and rolled in next to a very disagreeable fellow who didn't seem to appreciate having to share his straw sack. As the man moved, Father Bernard cringed at the very unpleasant odor that emanated from under the sheet. When he looked closer, he discovered the "sheet...caked with blood and pus."[193] Both of the man's calves were covered with phlegmons, or edemas filled with pus. In some people, hunger can cause ordinary swelling or edemas. In others, those edemas become gangrenous. Then they are called phlegmons. Generally, someone with that condition simply rots away. That evening, Father Bernard helped bandage the man's legs, but it took all his energy to stop from fainting.

Bandages were changed every Tuesday and Friday. Anyone who had an open sore was required to line up naked, even if the sore was on a finger, foot or hand, and walk to a table on which was laid some knives, a pair of scissors, a roll of paper for dressings, and a pot of salve. A prisoner who, just moments earlier, may have been sweeping the floor or doing some other unsanitary chore, was now assigned to the task of dressing wounds. These unhygienic conditions, coupled with the vitamin-poor diet and a general debility, meant that wounds never really healed at Dachau. Perhaps one of the most difficult and painful wound treatments was performed on those who had phlegmons. In that case, the attendant would

> "plunge a knife finger-deep into a badly swollen calf, and then repeat the process from the other side with another knife so that the two blades met somewhere in the leg. Blood, pus, and water would pour out [during each treatment]. After that a very long and thick needle was pushed through the whole calf with the blunt end and eye

143

first; a cloth soaked in a fluid was threaded into the eye and then pulled back through the wound by the pointed end of the needle. The rag was left in the wound so that it [didn't] close."[194]

The stench was so disgusting that most who could manage would run outside to escape it.

That night, the man next to Father Bernard kept ripping his bandages off. The odor was unbearable. Other men cursed and threatened the man, which of course did no good. Father Bernard had a weird feeling that night that someone was messing with his wounded neighbor. By morning, the man was dead. Father Bernard looked around the room and made eye contact with a man in the opposite bunk. He had the look of a madman. It turned out that he had strangled the priest's dead bunkmate during the night as a means of getting rid of the stench. Father Bernard didn't ask any questions. In reality, he was rather glad that the man would be removed.

On the third day in the infirmary, Batty Esch arrived. Esch shook Father Bernard's hand and told him that he had gotten beaten before being sent to the infirmary. "Brachmond is coming tomorrow, and then Wampach,"[195] Esch told Father Bernard. Batty was in bad shape and shared a middle bunk from the moment he arrived. The following day Brachmond arrived and was assigned to room one with Father Bernard and Batty. Father Wampach was given a bunk in room three when he arrived two days later.

One day, the order to "fall-in" was given to those in the infirmary and included the men incapable of standing. Immediately the worst possible speculation was aroused. The men were ordered to go outside and march in front of an SS officer while holding their medical charts in front of them. The indescribably vicious expression on the man's face unnerved Father Bernard, who figured it might be better at this point to feign good health. He summoned all his energy and marched by the officer standing perfectly straight. A few days later, about twenty men in the poorest of health were led away. They were not seen again. None of Father Bernard's friends were among the twenty.

About a week afterward, Brachmond developed phlegmons which, after just a few days, covered his entire body. The bandaging process left him looking like a mummy. The infirmary personnel called him "the ghost." The phlegmons on his head and neck, caused his greatest suffering and inflicted blinding headaches.

Father Bernard's time also came. The water retention in his feet moved up to his legs, and he developed edemas on his hands and face. The attendant commented that he looked like a bag of water. He wrote a big red W on the medical chart and moved him to a middle tier bunk.

Batty Esch, meanwhile, was suffering from dysentery. He tried desperately to "conceal it because men with that condition were labeled with an unvarnished term and moved immediately to room four where no one paid any more attention to their condition. If someone could no longer stand up, he just remained lying in his excrement until death released him." [196] Unfortunately, his bunkmate reported him, and he was sent immediately to room four. This only exacerbated Batty's depression.

Brachmond's condition also grew worse and was compounded by dysentery. His behavior declined to that of a child. Father Bernard tried to advise him, but his own condition had deteriorated to the point where he had great difficulty just standing up. One day, while trying to sneak into the toilet to wash out Brachmond's blanket, Father Bernard was caught. Brachmond was moved to room four within minutes. Father Bernard tried to offer words of consolation to him but was himself just moments away from a breakdown, and that happened a short time later.

Father Bernard was no longer in control of his speech. He managed his way back to his bunk and got under his blanket.

"All at once I had no contact with my surroundings. I had thoughts in my head, internal thoughts, but my thinking lacked concepts and seemed to me to have no influence on my external actions. I was incapable of coming up with even one verbal designation for something. In my mind I saw objects before me, and knew what they were., but I could not put a name to a single one.

While this was happening, I thought about the state I was in as if from the outside, as if I weren't involved. At first the thought came to me that I had died and was in eternity. Then I suddenly thought I had lost my mind. Still huddled under the blanket, I tried to whisper a few words, and I heard that I was talking nonsense.

Now I knew. I've gone crazy. It's all over..."[197]

It was about two hours later, when the feeling of being split in two was receding, that he heard a knock on a partially opened window next to his head. Batty Esch peered through and announced that Brachmond had died in his arms. Father Bernard couldn't stop crying until finally he regained his wits and prayed the *De Profundis* for his deceased friend.

The following day, an order was issued informing the infirmary personnel that priests were no longer eligible for medical treatment. Father Bernard learned of this order when he went to get his bandage changed. The order was later changed to allow priests to have dressings applied to their wounds. Father Bernard searched for the bright side; at least he would get his entire ladle of soup, he thought.

Over the course of time spent in the infirmary, Father Bernard noticed that all of barrack 7 was beginning to resemble the death block previously limited to room 4. The incurable from all the other wards were being sent there. These included those who suffered from "unclean, evil-smelling, or otherwise unpleasant ailments."[198] The population grew exponentially with inmates from the tuberculosis ward, twenty-two of them in all, being sent there. The patients suffering from this wildly communicable disease were not allowed to interact with the other infirmed patients as a means of keeping infection rates down, though that was relatively ineffective after the cross-contamination had occurred.

Despite his deteriorating health, Father Bernard was assigned to one of the upper bunks. That changed, however, when he established a cordial relationship with the young Polish man assigned to the room duty roster. Through his efforts, Father Bernard was finally moved to a first-tier bunk. His new bunkmate was also a priest, and the Pole thought it would be a more comfortable place for Father Bernard to die. The room duty clerk also advised the priest that the water build-up in his body might be treated with mercury injections, but they weren't available in barrack 7. Besides, priests were no longer allowed treatment, so it would be pointless to request assignment to another ward. The sympathetic clerk couldn't help but notice the disappointment that showed in Father

146

Bernard's face. He ran his hand over the priest's swollen body and said reassuringly, "It won't be today..."[199]

The following day, Father Bernard was unable to move. The fluid overtaking his body was impacting his heart. He knew instinctively that this would be his last day on earth. Through the window into room 4, he said his farewell to Batty Esch. His Polish bunkmate gave him absolution for the final time. Father Bernard closed his eyes, never before feeling closer to heaven. He turned his attention to his family in Luxembourg and then prayed to the Lord, quietly reciting "the long list of convictions for which [he] was willing to sacrifice [his] life for Him. As he prayed he faded into unconsciousness.

Father Bernard regained consciousness several hours later during the middle of the night. There were voices next to him. He could hear the whispering but didn't move a muscle. "Give it to me!" one man said. "You stupid idiot, that's the wrong injection!" "It doesn't matter," the other said, "there wasn't any other! And believe me, I'm not risking it a second time...."[200]

Just then the priest felt a pinch in his thigh, then a stabbing pain and before long, an alarming need to urinate. He slid slowly and deliberately to the ground and crawled on all fours to the toilet. The pain was dreadful. Once back in his bunk he was unable to sleep but needed to make additional trips to the toilet. By that point he felt fifteen or sixteen quarts lighter and knew intuitively that he would survive.

When morning finally arrived, he offered a word of thanks to his Polish clerk friend who insisted he did not know what the priest was talking about. Father Bernard never really found out if the clerk was denying his role out of caution or if someone else had intervened. It didn't matter, as Father Bernard was simply grateful for the new day.

When Batty appeared at the window, Father Bernard learned that the corpses were still stacked like firewood in room 4 with Father Brachmond laying at the bottom of the pile. This was camp procedure. Once the gold teeth were removed, the bodies were stacked until the crematorium commando carted them away.

As Father Bernard lay in his bunk thinking of all those who did not survive camp, he heard his number being called. "25487, come with me for interrogation." The man on duty advised him that the priest couldn't stand. "Then he can't be release either," the civilian Gestapo official standing in the doorway snapped. "Where is the son of a bitch?"[201]

With every ounce of energy that remained in his body, Father Bernard yelled, "Here!"[202] as he stood upright and wrapped a blanket around himself. He followed the official into the washroom and, at the official's command, took a seat on one of the toilets. "What would you do if you were released?" he said. "I would ask my bishop to grant me a leave of absence for health reasons," Bernard responded cautiously. "And then? Then you'd put your bleeding cassock back on, wouldn't you, and the whole masquerade would start all over again! I've heard enough," the officer said as he walked out the door.

Father Bernard made his way back to his bunk not really knowing what else he could have said. He couldn't denounce his faith or deny his Savior. He gave the best answer he could. A flood of responses entered his head, but it was too late now. He was disappointed but regretted nothing. At least someone, someplace was working on his release, he reasoned.

A few days passed and Father Bernard was feeling stronger. He was able to get up for a few hours each day, and spent that time sitting outside in the sun talking with Batty Esch.

Father Wampach was still confined to room 3 where a very strict attendant wouldn't allow his patients to have any contact with prisoners from the other rooms. They had no idea of his condition, but that soon changed when they learned that Wampach was being sent to the invalid block. That is where they sent prisoners still classified as unfit despite a stay in the infirmary. Invalid block was an alternative to the barrack and was segregated from the rest of the camp. In fact, a new regulation required that all priests leaving the infirmary, even those who were fit, would be assigned to the invalid block rather than returning to their barrack. The problem was that there was a regular flow of bodies from the invalid block to the crematorium. Generally speaking, once assigned to "the invalid block, one had little chance of remaining alive for more than a few weeks."[203]

Within a few days, Batty Esch got the call to invalid block. With Esch gone, Father Bernard began to spend more time with Father Maurice de Backer, who was from Brussels. He was deeply pious, and his positive attitude lifted Father Bernard's spirits. They spent a great deal of time together until July 23, when it was time for the two of them to leave the infirmary. They were able to walk albeit with a "shuffling gait and sluggish movements typical of [their] condition."[204] Together, they were marched off to the invalid block.

The influx of priests required that invalid block be expanded from one to three barracks, numbers 23, 25 and 27. As was the case with the infirmary, barbed-wire fencing separated the invalid block from the rest of the camp. In barrack 27, Father Bernard was reunited with his Luxembourg pals, Fathers Esch and Wampach and Monsignor Origer. The inmates were given only a shirt to wear and that had to be sewn together to form a single piece. Then they were assigned a room. Father Bernard and Monsignor Origer were sent to room 1. Esch and Wampach were placed in room 3.

Barrack 27 was devoid of any straw sack, and the inmates had to sleep on the wooden slats that spread across the bunks. The single blanket they were given could be used as either a mattress or a cover. Naturally, the new arrivals to the barrack were assigned the top bunk. Climbing to tier three was incredibly painful for Father Bernard who had to, with his hands, lift one knee to the foot end of the lower bunk; then, holding on to the foot of the middle bunk, pull himself up. This took all his strength but left him with only two knees on the foot of the bottom bunk. After a moment's rest, he used his hands to lift one foot to the bottom bunk then he used his arms to pull himself to a standing position with both feet resting on the bottom bunk. The entire process was repeated to lift himself to the middle and eventually to the top-tier bunk where he would fall onto the slats of wood that stretched across the two iron rods below. To his dismay, he discovered that one of his slats was missing requiring that the remaining slats be spread further apart to support the weight of his swollen body. With the loss of one of the wooden supports, there was always the danger of falling through to the bunk below. This process was repeated each and every time Father Bernard had to climb in or out of his bunk.

The daily routine in the invalid block was much less obtrusive than it was in the camp proper. The prisoners were still up by four o'clock but there was no requirement to fetch coffee. Rather, it was delivered at four-thirty. After coffee, the inmates were ordered out of the barrack until the midday meal. There was a private headcount on the barrack street where the inmates were allowed to stand, sit or lie regardless of the weather conditions. If sitting, prisoners were required to remove their wooden clogs and then sit on them with their arms around their knees. Leaning against the wall was strictly forbidden. This was most uncomfortable for those with boils or sores and they shifted position restlessly trying not to press their wounds against the hard gravel. Still, this was preferable to standing at attention for hours on end as was often the case in the priest barracks. Following the midday meal, the afternoon proceeded in the same fashion.

A new arrival to the invalid barrack was a Jesuit priest whom Father Bernard had known from the Catholic Film Bureau. Father de Coninck, because he had only recently arrived in Dachau, was still at relatively full strength. He quickly joined with Maurice de Backer and Father Bernard in a little spiritual and mental support group during this forsaken period of debilitation. The three would gather at an isolated portion of the barrack street and unobtrusively pray together. Of course, prayers would quickly turn to trivial talk if someone approached too closely. Following prayer, the three would sit and talk while sitting on their clogs and leaning back to back for support. Then, they would recite the "Mass" pulling from their collective memories.

Father de Coninck even had a small piece of consecrated Host that he smuggled in a cellophane bag of vitamin C. He had gotten it from a German priest in barrack 26 and Fathers Bernard and de Backer were almost giddy with excitement. Collectively they decided not to consume it immediately. Rather, each time they prayed "Mass" together, Father de Coninck clutched the Host inconspicuously in his hand. The consolation that the presence of Jesus; Body, Blood, Soul, and Divinity, brought to the hearts of the tormented priests, the amount of courage it gave them, and the readiness of their hearts to sacrifice, was beyond expression.

Every day and night, between fifty and one-hundred prisoners housed in the invalid block were selected for "transport." This was essentially a death march to the gas chamber. There was no rhyme or reason to the selection. It seemed to be random. Some men grumbled as they lined up, while others expressed bitter distress. Some displayed no emotion at all when the command was given to march.

On Saturday, August 1, 1942, Father Bernard received the distressing news that his name was on the "transport" list. While there was no news about the others, Father Bernard was scheduled for transport on the following Saturday. The university students who brought the news, all members of the Catholic Action group in Vienna, told him that Father Schmitz said that he could buy their names off the list. "Someone is prepared to switch your names from the list of the living to the dead in the card file. Then you'll never be called up for transport. The price is one and a half loaves of bread."[205]

Father Bernard promised his answer by the following day and rushed off to tell the others. He could find no consensus among them, however. Wampach thought the price was too high noting that he couldn't possibly save a loaf and a half of bread in one week. Besides, he added, what is the difference if we die in the gas chamber or of starvation. Father Bernard had no choice however, as he was already on the transport list. Batty Esch said he would help him if Father Bernard would then return the favor. The two agreed. "I'll help both of you," added Monsignor Origer. "I demand nothing more from life. My work is done."[206] The gesture of sacrifice that the two men made would later move Father Bernard to tears, but on that Saturday, they simply shook hands without saying a word.

The following day, Fathers Bernard and Esch met the students at the barbed-wire fence and gave them a half loaf of bread along with their answer. The half loaf, which constituted a down payment, had to be broken into smaller pieces that could pass through the openings in the fence. The students, in turn, told them that the first name would disappear from the card file of living inmates. The priests left with an uneasy feeling knowing that if the person altering the records was found out, it would mean certain death for both him and the priest he was trying to save. It mattered little to Father Bernard, however, who was already slated to die in just six days.

Also of concern to Father Bernard was that fact that his name would, from that day forward, be listed among the dead. That might be problematic if he did become eligible for release. But, the potential for release prior to the following Saturday seemed a remote possibility at best.

The next few nights were spent in sleepless anticipation and his days in restless anxiety. He thought of all that could go wrong with the card transfer and began to focus more on the process of dying. He tried in vain to pray, but the distractions overtook him.

Father Bernard's Release from Dachau
August 5, 1942

On Wednesday, August 5, 1942, Father Bernard and the other inmates of invalid block fell in for morning head count. He found himself directly behind Baron X from Paris, who was suffering from diarrhea. The watery contents of his bowels ran down his leg, and the man standing aside of him cursed about the stench and punched him in the gut. Father Bernard had just about finished his verbal chastisement of the insensitive man when the SS officer arrived for the count. Suddenly the thought of release flashed through Father Bernard's mind. If his release were to be achieved, it would have to be on this day. As the thought ran through his mind, someone called out, "25487."

For a moment, he was frozen in place but the curses from the SS officer and the barrack head prisoner, as well as the kick of envy from one of the other inmates, broke the binds of his paralysis. He stumbled to the front of the group and looked around, without success, for his friends. He was handed a pair of trousers to complete his dress and was accompanied to the camp street. Following the SS man proved too strenuous a task however, and Father Bernard collapsed in the street while the guard went to retrieve another inmate from barrack 25. Within minutes, an old, crippled man, who had been sent to camp by mistake just a few days earlier, appeared at the door and joined the priest in the street. Father Bernard leaned on the old man pretending to help him walk. He needed to keep up appearances of good health because severely debilitated prisoners were not allowed to be released. But Father Bernard grew weaker with every step and was certain, as the entourage approached the infirmary, that he simply wouldn't pass the doctor's inspection.

The priest's guardian angel must have been working overtime, however, as the SS doctor was not in when they arrived at the infirmary, and the task of inspection fell to his acting deputy, a prisoner, who protested that he was not authorized to sign release certificates. The SS officer would hear none of it. "Listen here, you son of a bitch! This is my day off. Do you think I'm going to stand around with these two guys all afternoon? You fill out those forms right now and stamp them, understand? Whatever lies you have to tell the doctor is your problem!"[207] He emphasized his demand with a quick punch to the attendant's head.

The unfortunate prisoner opened the record book as Father Bernard undressed and stepped on the scale. He was just over one hundred pounds. The SS officer wouldn't allow the attendant to look and told him to write one-hundred-and-fifty pounds in the record. "And top fit," he added. "No open soars, no lice, no scabies. Well nourished, and in great shape overall!"[208]

Within just seconds the men were back on the street and Father Bernard finally had a good feeling about the reality of his release. His clothes, relinquished eighteen months earlier upon his arrival, were returned to him as was his money. Nothing was missing. He was given the usual warning in the political office and told that his release was probationary. "You will remain in protective custody and must report every second day to the security police in Luxembourg until the end of the war!" The restrictions suited Father Bernard just fine.

Standing outside the main gate, still in the company of a guard, a small van arrived and took them to the train station. Once they arrived at the station Father Bernard asked permission to go to the post office across the street to send a telegram to his family, then he returned to the station and, with assistance, boarded his train. A female conductor found a seat for him on the overcrowded train, but it wasn't until the train pulled away from the station that he felt truly free. He was now free to do whatever he wanted, and the thought of that sovereignty was difficult to comprehend.

The next morning, Thursday, August 6, 1942, Father Bernard stood at the altar again for the first time. It was the anniversary of the day he had first celebrated Mass. He would not stand there again for a very long time as he suffered a total collapse of his health.

Chapter 11

Liberation

Father Jean Bernard was released on probation after being incarcerated at the Dachau concentration camp for one year, two months and seventeen days. Weighing barely one-hundred pounds, he spent a "year in a sanitorium in a state of extreme debility and exhaustion. [He was] constantly bothered by the Gestapo in Luxembourg, who clearly resented being bypassed on the matter of his release."[209] Following his discharge from the sanitorium, Father Bernard relocated to a monastery where he was finally liberated by Allied forces in October 1944. He immediately returned to work in the film area and served as editor of the *Luxembourg Wort,* the Catholic daily newspaper. In 1947 Father Bernard was elected president of the International Catholic Cinema Office and remained in that office until his memoir was published as a book in 1962. He later served as a consultant to the Papal Commission for Film, Radio and Television. He was also a member of the Preparatory Secretariat for the Press and the Entertainment World in advance of the Second Vatican Council. Father Bernard died on September 1, 1994, at the age of eighty-seven.

At the time of his probationary release in early August 1942, tens of thousands of others remained in the impounds of Dachau and the numerous other concentration camps within the network of Nazi torture chambers for many more months. Father Bernard endured the unremitting torments of camp life during his time at Dachau, but many who were alive at the time of Father Bernard's release did not survive while they waited for the Allied forces to appear and liberate the camps. It took another two years for the Axis fortunes to change and for the Allied powers to arrive.

Though every day at Dachau was torment, it was during the final months before liberation that the prisoners suffered most. In addition to the lack of food, extraordinary work assignments and outrageous disciplinary measures that were routine at the camp, an epidemic of louse-borne typhus ravaged the compound. Combined with a reduction of incoming mail, and the overcrowding that resulted from the transport of prisoners from other camps, the inmates suffered terrible physical, emotional and psychological pain.

The end for Germany may have begun as early as late 1942. At Hitler's insistence, Germany and the Axis powers began to invade the Soviet Union starting at the end of June and lasting through September 1942. This turned out to be a fatal mistake for the Third Reich as the Soviets launched a counterattack which resulted in the surrender of Germany's Sixth Army by the end of the year. By mid-May 1943 the Axis forces had surrendered in Tunisia bringing an end to the North African campaign, and by mid-August, Allied forces took control of Sicily and deposed Fascist leader Benito Mussolini. Less than two months later, Sicily surrendered to the Allied powers. Despite attempts to take and occupy Rome, Allied forces liberated that city on June 4, 1944.

Meanwhile, the United States had launched a reign of terror on Germany beginning in April 1944. More than seven-hundred U.S. bombers, accompanied by more than eight-hundred fighter aircraft, bombed several major cities in Germany. Then, on January 28, 1945, following the Allied victory in the Battle of the Bulge, the German Army was forced to retreat within the original boundaries of Germany.

The Battle of Iwo Jima began on February 13 with the U.S. Navy bombardment of the island for three consecutive days leading up to the U.S. Marine invasion. Within ten days, U.S. forces took the island and planted its flag on the summit of Mount Suribachi. Axis powers were falling everywhere, and it appeared the days of the Third Reich were numbered.

The prisoners at Dachau, meanwhile, were of the belief that the highest-ranking SS officers had given orders to exterminate every prisoner in camp. True or not, the inmates believed the rumors and were in a frenzied state. One rumor circulating in the camp was that the inmates would be killed using flamethrowers or by bombs dropped from the sky. There may have been actual discussion of that sort among the SS who were plotting a bombardment on their own facilities, one that they could blame on the Allied forces. The rumors were as rampant in the clergy barracks as throughout the general population of inmates, but the priests found strength in prayer. Father Hoffmann affirmed:

> "From February 3 to 11, 1945, special divine offices were celebrated in the chapel to avert dangers. Typhus was raging at Dachau. The bombardments threatened the camp, and there were many other dangers. During these devotions the priest prayed not only for themselves but also for the detainees. Every evening Father de Coninck provided a meditation in Latin. Then the litanies and prayers followed, conducted in turn by priests of different nationalities."[210]

Perhaps the prayers bore fruit, as just about two weeks later, beginning on March 27 and continuing through April 11, priests were released from Dachau in large numbers. Those released numbered almost one-hundred-and fifty and were all of German or Austrian descent. Clearly, if the German plan was to remove all evidence of the concentration camp, the release of priests would not achieve that objective. Those released didn't forget about the suffering of their compatriots either.

> "Among the liberated priests were several well-known individuals, such as the chaplain Georg Schelling; Father Otto Pies; Pallotine Father Josef Kentenich, founder of the Schoenstatt Movement; and Father Corbinian Hofmeister, Abbot of the Benedictine Abbey in Metten, who was detained in the bunker of honor. Some of the liberated priests displayed a remarkable devotion, such as Father Josef Neunzig – nicknamed 'Jupp' by his fellow detainees – who came back to the plantation shop dressed in civilian clothing to bring provisions secretly to those who were still behind the barbed-wire fences. Some of

them died after a few weeks – for example, Father Peter Schlicker, who died of typhus on April 19 in the hospital in Salzburg. Father Johannes Zimmermann, freed on March 29, was run over by a car on July 25, 1945, and did not survive his injuries."[211]

Despite the German losses, the horrors of the war raged on. In early April, U.S. troops took Okinawa, the last island held by the Japanese, and this was followed by the Russian capture of Vienna. The series of Allied victories led to an end to German resistance, which resulted in three-hundred-and-seventy-thousand German prisoners of war being interned. Hitler remained in Berlin and on April 25, 1945, American and British troops converged at Torgau in Germany, sealing the fate of the Third Reich.

As "Allied and Soviet troops moved across Europe against Nazi Germany in 1944 and 1945, they encountered concentration camps, mass graves, and other sites of Nazi crimes. The unspeakable conditions the liberators confronted shed light on the full scope of Nazi horrors."[212]

The first major camp to be liberated was Majdanek in Lublin, Poland. Soviet forces freed the prisoners from that camp during their westward advance. Unfortunately, the SS had evacuated most of the camp a few months before the Soviets arrived with the majority of prisoners being sent to camps such as Gross-Rosen, Auschwitz and Mauthausen. Despite the Nazi efforts at concealment, the camp was basically intact and a number of prisoners, mostly Soviet POWs, were still there when the Soviets arrived on the night of July 22. The Soviets "also encountered substantial evidence of the mass murder committed at Majdanek by Nazi Germans."[213] In addition to Majdanek, Soviet forces liberated Stutthof, Sahsenhausen, and Ravensbrück.

Perhaps sensing defeat, Heinrich Himmler issued an order to evacuate and relocate all concentration camp prisoners to camps located in the interior of Germany. The resulting overcrowding in the German camps was of little consequence to the SS who, at this point, could probably see the writing on the wall. Most of the transports of prisoners evacuated from other outlying camps arrived at Dachau, and the trains arrived on a near continual basis. After days of travel with little to nothing to eat or drink, the prisoners

Liberators found dead bodies both inside and outside of the camp's grounds.
(Source: Report on the Liberation of Dachau.)

arrived weak and near death. Many, in fact, died during transport, and their bodies were left rotting on the train. Consequently, due to the overcrowding and lack of sanitary conditions, typhus epidemics blossomed both on the death train and in camp. "The most lethal of these convoys arrived in Dachau on April 28. It had left Buchenwald three weeks before, and it included several religious."[214]

As U.S. troops approached the city, Dachau experienced a constant flow of alerts. The Crematoria couldn't incinerate the dead fast enough, and bodies were stockpiled in buildings and ditches and on the transport trains. By April 26, 1945 there were 67,665 prisoners registered at Dachau and its subcamps. In a desperate attempt to eliminate evidence of Nazi terrorism, the SS organized a march of a column of more than seven-thousand prisoners from Dachau to the southern town of Tegernsee, a distance of almost forty-five miles. The column contained 1,524 Jews, 4,150 Russians, and 1,213 Reichsdeutsche, among whom were almost one-hundred priests. Many in the column perished along the way from hunger, exhaustion or exposure to the elements. Those who were too tired or weak to continue the march were simply shot where they fell.

Father Otto Pies tried to assist the prisoners. He wrote:

"I was able to save many confreres, many priests who participated in the 'death march' of the 7,000 detainees from Dachau, a desperate, horrifying convoy traveling at night. During this rescue operation, our students from the scholasticate worked wonders, particularly Brother Franz Kreis, who was a lieutenant in the army. Father von Tatenback, the rector, and Father Kormann put the institution's truck at my disposal; they procured foodstuffs for the detainees who were dying of hunger during that march; courageously and bodily they welcomed those who were successfully saved, either in their house or in the neighborhood."[215]

At camp, conditions were changing rapidly. On the morning of Sunday, April 29, the camp seemed devoid of guards. Most, of the SS had deserted except for the few who remained at their post in the watchtowers. Just before Noon, while returning from Sunday services, the priests noticed that a white flag had been unfurled within the camp. This certainly was encouraging, but they also knew that the German flamethrowers could incinerate everyone in camp before the Allied forces arrived. The clergymen retreated to the chapel where one Mass followed another for the entire day. In the late afternoon, the first wave of American forces arrived at camp.

"According to several testimonies, the first three Americans to enter the camp were a Jewish soldier, Samuel Kahn; a woman journalist, Margaret Higgins; and a military chaplain, who recited the Our Father from the Jourhaus and then invited the crowd of detainees to pray for their former executioners."[216]

Despite the attempt to remove seven-thousand prisoners from the camp, Dachau still held more than sixty-thousand inmates in a facility intended to hold only about ten thousand. Every day, thousands more died and were piled up awaiting room at the crematorium. Father Jacques Sommet described all the bodies strewn among the camp as "[A] human carpet. A mass grave was dug behind the plantation in an unsuccessful attempt to absorb the surplus cadavers."[217] From the first day of 1945 until liberation almost four months later, approximately fourteen-thousand people perished at Dachau alone.

Dachau was the last major camp liberated* and therefore SS officials had the most time to destroy many of the camp records that might have been used as evidence against them in any subsequent war-crime

One of the many rail cars filled with prisoner corpses that was discovered by American forces upon the surrender of Dachau on April 29, 1945. (Photo credit: United States Holocaust Memorial Museum)

---

*Ravensruck, a satellite camp of Dachau was the primary facility used for the storage of prisoner's clothing, was liberated on April 30. Mauthausen, which was initially a satellite camp of Dachau, but later became an independent camp, was the last camp liberated several days later on May 5.

The United States Holocaust Memorial Museum, Liberation of Nazi Camps.

trials. On Sunday, April 29, 1945, American Army forces from the 42nd and 45th Infantry Division moved in from different directions and the camp was surrendered to them by Sturmschaführer Heinrich Wicker. U.S. Brig. General Henning Linden described the surrender in his official "Report on the Surrender of Dachau Concentration Camp:"

> "As we moved down along the west side of the concentration camp and approached the southwest corner, three people approached down the road under a flag of truce. We met these people about 75 yards north of the southwest entrance to the camp. These three people were a Swiss Red Cross representative and two SS troopers who said they were the camp commander and assistant camp commander and that they had come into the camp on the night of the 28th to take over from the regular camp personnel for the purpose of turning the camp over to the advancing Americans. The Swiss Red Cross representative acted as interpreter and stated that there were about 100 SS guards in the camp who had their arms stacked except for the people in the tower. He said he had given instructions that there would be no shots fired and it would take about 50 men to relieve the guards, as there were 42,000 half-crazed prisoners of war in the camp, many of them typhus infected. He asked if I were an officer of the American army, to which I replied, 'Yes, I am Assistant Division Commander of the 42d Division and will accept the surrender of the camp in the name of the Rainbow Division for the American army.'"[218]

US soldiers found more than thirty rail cars filled with decaying bodies. They also discovered more than thirty-two-thousand prisoners packed into thirty barracks. The SS had crammed sixteen-hundred men into a barrack intended to support only two-hundred-and-fifty men maximum. Soldiers liberated about thirty-thousand prisoners in early May. Another roughly thirty-thousand were dead.

As the liberators surveyed the camp, they were horrified at the site of the starving prisoners, the piles of bodies in the barracks, in the yard and in the train cars. Despite the white flag hanging in the camp, some SS men refused to surrender their weapons. They were very quickly shot by the American soldiers. At one point, perhaps acting out of a sense of rage at what they had just witnessed, the U.S. troops lined up several camp guards against a wall and unceremoniously executed them.

"Some detainees pursued their executioners through the camp. Mansarian, one of the most sadistic capos, of Armenian descent, was dragged from his hiding place by his victims. The man was stoned and almost torn apart. His body joined the lineup of SS cadavers."

The reaction of Dachau prisoners after liberation of the camp by Allied forces was overwhelming for many of the liberators. (Source: Report on the Liberation of Dachau.)

Despite some of these select acts of rage, most in camp were euphoric. Shouts of joy from prisoners could be heard throughout the camp and some hung their nation's flag from the rooftops.

> "Father Rene Fraysse mentions a 'formidable joy. An Easter joy of the Resurrection.' A Te Deum was celebrated at the chapel at the end of the day. In Blocks 26 and 28, the reactions were varied. Jacques Sommet went to the crematorium. 'Then simply, without thinking about it, I just started to recite the Our Father for those who were resting there.'"[219]

The very next day, April 30, 1945, with Soviet troops just outside of his bunker, Adolf Hitler used his own pistol to fire one bullet into his brain. The madman who nearly destroyed the world and was responsible for the near extermination of an entire race of people was dead. Along with him were buried his grand plans and designs for an Arian Nation. But for hundreds of thousands of survivors, nothing, certainly not life, would ever be the same.

Conclusion

Notwithstanding their liberation, the horrors for those who had endured unspeakable torment at the hands of the Nazis had not yet ended at Dachau. The American liberators were totally unprepared to deal with the typhus outbreak at the camp, and without a plan, they simply quarantined all the detainees. Afraid to release infected prisoners into the general population, American troops were forced to replace the SS as new camp administrators until a solution could be worked out. The detainees were granted an internal autonomy but remained under the close scrutiny of their American liberators. Over the course of the next few days, the American medical corps deployed potential remedies; a massive camp dusting with DDT and a vaccination program. Regardless, typhus remained as virulent as before. During the month of May, another 2,221 detainees perished at Dachau. Most deaths were attributable to typhus, while a few detainees simply did not survive the sudden change of diet, succumbing shortly after eating a pound of canned pork or beef.

Like before, the bodies had still not been removed, not so much because there was no capacity to bury them, but rather because the Americans seemed intent to exploit the images for propaganda's sake. Photographers were frequent visitors to the camp taking photographs and film-newsreel footage of the cadavers, all to the shock of the detainees. "Some in the clergy petitioned the American authorities to improve the lot of their comrades, to let them leave the barbed-wire enclosure and to house them in the SS quarters."[220]

Father Michel Riquet was among those who protested. In a letter to Allied forces commander General Dwight Eisenhower, Riquet wrote:

164

"You will understand our impatience and even our astonishment at the fact that, more than ten days after greeting our liberators, the 34,000 detainees of Dachau are still prisoners of the same barbed-wire fences, guarded by sentinels whose orders are still to fire on anyone who attempts to escape – which for every prisoner is a natural right, especially when he is told that he is free and victorious. In the barracks that are visited every day by the international press, some men continue to stagnate, stacked in these triple-decker beds that dysentery turns into a filthy cesspool, while the lanes between the blocks continue to be lined with cadavers – 135 per day – just like in the darker times of the tyranny that you conquered."[221]

The typhus epidemic was finally in check by early June and the process of repatriation of the detainees began. First the Belgians, Luxembourgers, and Dutchmen were released, followed by the French. Finally, the Polish, who were still fearful of returning to their homeland now under Communist control. Several Poles "headed for Paris instead, where they were welcomed by Archbishop Emmanuel Cardinal Suhard and Apostolic Nuncio Angelo Roncalli, who would later become Pope John XXIII. Some who had been waiting for several years for priestly ordination behind the barbed wire of Dachau became priests as early as the summer of 1945."[222]

Epilogue

"It would be easier for the world to survive without the sun than to do without holy mass."

-Padre Pio

I t is widely accepted that during the time of the Third Reich, Adolph Hitler was responsible for the extermination of some six million Jews, or about two-thirds of the mid-twentieth-century European Jewish population. It is also a well-known historical fact that Hitler's Reich targeted several other groups such as Poles, Communists, the disabled, asocials, criminals, political opponents of any strife, Jehovah's witnesses, homosexuals, and gypsies, with the ultimate goal of creating one Aryan master race.

Far less examined, however, is the fact that Hitler's Nazi Germany was also opposed to the propagation of religion and as such endeavored to bring about the elimination of all major beliefs, including the Catholic faith. Although the Nazi Party made no illusion of its disdain for Catholicism, and despite the Party's overt attacks on the Catholic Church during the 1930s and 1940s, the impact of the Reich on the Church is seldom discussed.

Despite the lack of discourse, the fact remains that millions of Catholics were targeted and many were killed during Hitler's reign of terror. In Poland alone, "Between 1939 and 1945, at least one–and-a-half million Polish citizens [a great many of them Catholics] were deported to German territory into forced labor. Hundreds of thousands were also imprisoned in Nazi concentration camps."223 During those years, Catholics accounted for about 71 percent of Poland's population. That number has steadily risen since then and,

166

in 2020, the people of that nation were 88 percent Catholic. "Half of Poland's Catholic priests, monks, and nuns suffered repression during the six long years of World War II,"[224] with more than 2,800 killed at Nazi and Soviet hands. According to Anna Jagodzinska of Poland's National Remembrance Institute, "clergy were particularly targeted as upholders of national culture and identity."[225]

Piles of bodies of prisoners killed just before liberation were found throughout the camp. (Source: Report on the Liberation of Dachau.)

Life in Dachau, as was the case in any of the Third Reich concentration camps, was a living hell for every prisoner who entered its gates. It is certain that none of the prisoners wanted to be there and every aspect of camp life was meant to be a torturous experience. But the Catholic priests of Dachau had an additional burden. They were charged by their ministry with bringing God and the Good News to the others. It was their sacred obligation to hear the prisoner's confessions, to administer the last rites of the Church to the dying, to show mercy and compassion to all, including their tormentors, and to do everything within their power to brighten the otherwise bleakness that each new day resurrected all while suffering the same fate as those they were to comfort. It was never an easy task and, at times, they failed. But every day brought a new opportunity to bring both the message and the persona of Jesus to the camp. To do so, they risked their own daily rations, excruciating beatings, hangings on the tree, and even death. But each day, they took that risk because providing pastoral services and spiritual care to others, well, that was their sacred duty, and they tried their best to do it every day despite their own sufferings and hardships. How far would you go to do the right thing in the face of torture and death? Maximilian Kolbe went the extra mile of substituting himself for a man scheduled to die by starvation and dehydration. "No greater love than this," Jesus told us, "than to lay down one's life for a friend."[226]

Despite Hitler's efforts to obliterate Christianity, the religion still flourishes worldwide almost eighty years later. Though still oppressed in various parts of the world, and under more subtle forms of attack in many other places, it remains one of the most prominent religions in society today.

The attempt by Adolf Hitler and his men of the Third Reich to destroy religion represents only one of the many external threats to Christianity since its formation some two-thousand years ago. The world was warned, however, of an internal threat that is much more dangerous and of significantly greater consequence to the Church. That threat, alluded to in the New Testament, was emphatically reinforced in one of the best-known and most beloved of the Marian apparitions...Her appearance to the three shepherd children in Fatima, Portugal, more than one-hundred years ago.

In 1917 the Blessed Virgin Mary warned the children of a coming apostasy that would nearly cripple the church in the later part of the twentieth century, and indeed, time has proven Her correct. While Communists and Free Masons infiltrated the highest levels of the Catholic Church in the middle part of the century relaxing long-held traditions, issuing confusing statements, and creating controversy from within, the Church has seen a steady decline in the number of parishioners and a deterioration of the dogma in the hearts and minds of the faithful, a decline that not even Adolf Hitler and his Third Reich could have dreamed possible.

Today the church is undergoing dual attacks. The traditional progressive assaults that emanate from outside of the Church are ever present and gaining strength through euphemistic promotions, demagoguery, and propaganda. That effort is reinforced by a new internal threat that, as the Blessed Virgin Mary predicted, has infiltrated the highest levels of the Church.

There are many examples of the external threats that have plagued the Church. It began more than a half century ago with the decision by the Supreme Court of the United States (SCOTUS) to remove prayer from schools in June 1962. That decision was followed by others that banned Bible reading in 1963, legalized abortions on demand in 1973, and approved the display of offensive and blasphemous art in 1987 and 1996. All considered, there have been an unprecedented number of anti-Christian Supreme Court rulings in the twenty-first century.

There is one example, however, that conflates both the external and the internal threats to the Church. The worldwide response to the Covid-19 pandemic of 2020 led to the radical closure of churches and the altering of many of the faith's cherished traditions and sacramentals.

It was not the external pressure by government that was so shocking, however. As noted, that pressure has been a consistent force against Christianity since the mid-twentieth century. Rather, it was the acquiescence, support, and assistance to this assault, offered by some within the Church hierarchy, that enabled the Church to shut its doors, that was so disturbing. The closing of churches in the United States for three to eight months in the early part of 2020 was unparalleled in this country and devastating to those Catholics who were denied all the sacraments, including the most vital sacraments of Confession and the Holy Eucharist.

To Catholics, the Eucharist is the real presence of Jesus, Body, Blood, Soul and Divinity, and regular reception is sacrosanct. In order for a Catholic to receive the precious Body and Blood, one must be in a state of grace, a state attained only after making a sincere and complete confession of mortal sins to a priest. Denying a devout Catholic these sacraments is spiritually and emotionally unacceptable. To add insult to injury, when the government eventually allowed churches to reopen, permission was granted to reopen at rates below the level at which many other businesses were allowed to do so. For example, restaurants, in many cases, were allowed to reopen at up to fifty-percent capacity while churches could attain only a five- to twenty-five-person capacity depending on jurisdiction. In San Francisco, while the government allowed many businesses to operate at fifty-percent capacity, all churches were restricted to five *people* at a time, despite the fact that some churches were large enough to accommodate up to twelve-hundred people. Even outdoor church services were restricted to between fifty to one-hundred people while outdoor gatherings of protesters were unlimited in size, devoid of social distancing and featuringmany protesters without masks. Worse, these protests were attended and supported by the same elected officials responsible for imposing the restrictions on churches.

Archbishop Charles Chaput, Archbishop Emeritus of Philadelphia, said that "While some Church leaders fought to keep their churches open, some Catholic bishops were 'too compliant' with state and local restrictions on churches during the recent pandemic. If you don't reach out to people who are lonely and suffering and dying in a time like the pandemic, then you're not being the Church, and that's very, very bad for everyone involved."[227] Chaput noted that he was "sympathetic to the situation of bishops and other Church leaders, because it is an essential part of Christianity to be 'cooperative' in order to serve the common good. But as time went on and leaders saw the effect of this on their churches, it seems to me that they should have been more insistent on being available to the people who needed their care."[228]

Chaput, whose father was a mortician, released a new book, *Things Worth Dying For: Thoughts on a Life Worth Living,* in early 2021. In it, the retired bishop notes that "What we're willing to die for reveals what we're willing to live for, the things we really hold as sacred – not just with our words, but with our hearts...A good death can only be had as the fruit of a good life, a life lived with integrity and right purpose."[229]

Speaking in an interview in June 2021, Archbishop Chaput, when asked how closing churches and suspending public Masses, affected the faithful, answered, "We're beginning to discover that many people discovered that they don't need to go to church," adding, "but they did not feel any different not going than when they went."[230]

Now there are those who would argue that the public health was at stake from a novel coronavirus that reached pandemic proportions in early 2020, and that it was necessary for churches to close to stop the spread of a deadly disease. This argument is specious for many reasons, however. First, there is absolutely no evidence that the virus was spread in churches in America. Most Catholic churches, for example, voluntarily sanitized every pew, door and common area after each Mass. They eliminated liturgical books from the pews, removed sacramentals such as Holy Water from the fonts, required those attending to wear masks, and enforced social-distancing standards by roping off every other pew and limited those in a single pew to members of the same family. Second, at the height of the pandemic, the virus carried with it a death rate of less than three percent in the United States[231] and barely three percent worldwide. The U.S. death rate was above the national average in a handful of states, but most of those were states with an extremely high elderly population and, in those states, most of the deaths beyond the three percent average occurred in nursing homes due to a mishandling of the infected persons. Third, there is some evidence that the Covid-19-related death rate may have been inflated. Fourth, every Catholic had the option of sheltering in place, even if the churches had been allowed to remain open, because they were given a blanket dispensation from the requirement to attend Mass from the various bishops throughout the country. Consequently, those who were vulnerable or afraid had no need to risk infection for the sake of conformance to the laws of the Church. But whether or not the pandemic constituted a public health disaster is of lesser consequence to the greater issue of the faithful's spiritual need for the Church and its sacraments.

This is not to make light of the severity of the pandemic. Clearly, many people died as a result of this virus. Many more suffered significantly. The impact of Covid-19 should not be minimized, and government's reaction in closing nonessential businesses in an attempt to contain the virus, may have been warranted and justified. That is a question that will probably be debated for many years, yet it is a separate question than the one addressed here. The point of this discourse is whether this, or any crisis, would warrant the closure of churches and the separation of the faithful from the sacraments. To those who need their faith nourished with the sacraments, church is not nonessential, but rather intensely essential to their spiritual growth and well-being.

During the months of the closure, sacraments were denied to the faithful despite the overwhelming need for them. During those initial months of the pandemic, when the churches remained closed, tens of thousands of Catholics died without benefit of receiving the anointing of the sick or the last rites. Many Catholics were buried without benefit of a Catholic Mass, but rather Catholics were forced to bury their loved ones after a "service," limited to only 5 to 25 family members depending on the region. For months, millions of Catholics were denied daily or weekly reception of the Holy Eucharist as well as the sacrament of confession. Thousands of young Catholics were unable to make their First Confession, their First Holy Communion, or their Confirmation. The administration of those sacraments was postponed, which forced the anticipating participants to wait months before another opportunity was offered. And all of this was done in the name of the protection of public health without regard to the protection of the spiritual health – the primary concern of the Church. In that sense, closing the churches betrayed the faithful and ran afoul of sacred tradition.

The Christian example of risking everything for the purpose of the propagation of the faith has been demonstrated clearly throughout history. Jesus Himself ministered to the sick and diseased people. He cured lepers and healed the infirmed without regard to the potential spread of germs, despite the communicable nature of diseases such as leprosy.

The early Christians were faced with far greater external threats to their health and well-being. Such is the case even today in China and in other communist, socialist, and Islamic nations, where the practice of Christianity has been outlawed and Christians, if caught, are imprisoned, tortured, and killed. Regardless of the consequences, those Christians were willing to risk persecution and death. Why?

The Twelve Apostles knew Jesus. They walked with Him and witnessed His miracles. They ate with Him and some saw Him transfigured. They prayed with Him, and He appeared to them after He resurrected. They knew, beyond all doubt, that He was the Messiah, the Chosen One, the Son of God. Therefore, when faced with a choice of denying Him or building His Church, they chose to remain loyal, despite the risk of having to suffer long, cruel, and horribly painful deaths. They didn't worry about the personal consequences to their health and well-being. They were concerned only about spreading the faith through example, even the example of their own hideous deaths.

Christians are aware that Judas Iscariot, the Apostle who betrayed Jesus, committed suicide and died believing that his sin was far too grievous to ever be forgiven by God. John, the beloved Apostle, was not martyred, but instead exiled. He was banished to the Greek Island of Patmos where he died at an old age and in relative seclusion. The others, however, stood strong in the face of unmitigated brutality and suffered the harshest consequences for their faith.

They also preached openly despite threats from Jewish leaders and Roman officials. Peter, the man Jesus chose to lead His Church, was crucified. The brutality of Roman crucifixion is well known from Biblical accounts and other historic writings. The humiliation of being stripped naked and tied or nailed to a cross was almost beyond human endurance, but Peter volunteered to make the experience even worse. Thinking himself unworthy to die in the same manner as did his Savior, Peter asked to be crucified upside down. The Romans were happy to oblige him in that quest and probably extracted a great deal of satisfaction watching the animals nipping at Peter's face as he lay helplessly, straddled to the cross.

Peter's brother Andrew was also crucified. He too "asked to be nailed to a cross different from the Cross of Jesus. In his case it was a diagonal or X-shaped cross from which he was hung. That cross has thus come to be known as 'St. Andrew's cross.'"[232]

The description of the brutal death of the Apostle James the Lesser was provided by the Jewish historian Flavius Josephus in his work known as the *Jewish Antiquities*. In those pages he wrote, "The death of James was decided with an illegal initiative by the High Priest Ananus, a son of the Ananias attested to in the Gospels; in the year 62, he profited from the gap between the deposition of one Roman prosecutor (Festus) and the arrival of his successor (Albinus), to hand James over for stoning."[233] Being stoned may not sound like the most gruesome way to die, but the Roman method of stoning was extraordinarily painful. The condemned was generally placed against a wall where piles of stones lay ready to be thrown. Unlike modern depictions of a stoning, where someone stands above the head of the victim with a large stone ready to instantaneously crush the victim's skull, the stones used in this style of execution were large enough that they would cause life-threatening damage, but not so big as to kill the victim on impact. The stoning process was meant to cause a slow, painful, and deliberate death. Good executioners could make it last thirty minutes or more. Each minute, the victim withstood tens of large stones pummeling his body, each capable of breaking blood vessels and bones and causing internal bleeding and trauma severe enough to cause his eventual death.

Perhaps one of the worst types of martyrdom experienced by an Apostle at the hands of anti-Christian persecutors was flaying. This was the type of torture inflicted upon St. Luke. The purpose of flaying was to create as much pain as feasible for the victim, while the torturer skillfully worked to make the pain and suffering last as long as possible. Flaying, by nature, is a long, excruciating process that could last from hours to days. This form of punishment dates to about 900 BC and, over time, as it made its way around the world, was perfected as a means of execution.

As with all victims of flaying, the torturous death that St. Luke endured for the sake of his faith started with preparation of his skin so that it would become softened and thereby easier to cut through. This could have been done in a variety of ways, but two very common methods were to leave the victim tied down in the sun until the skin was burnt significantly. Another method was to place the victim in boiling water for a brief time. Either way, the skin became soft and pliable and simpler to cut and peel.

Before the flaying even began, therefore, the victim would already be in excruciating pain. Next, St. Luke's hands and feet would have been spread and tied to a table rendering him immobile. Chances are that he actually was forced to watch as the flayer sharpened the knife that would be used to slice through his skin. The persecutor would then use that knife to make long incisions in a rectangular fashion somewhere on the body, quite possibly on the thigh or buttocks. If the torturer wanted to inflict the maximum pain, the incision would be made along the face where there is a greater concentration of nerve receptors.

The goal of the torturer was to get the largest pieces of skin off intact because that skin was often hung on doors as a means of threatening others with the same torture if they persisted in their "unacceptable" behavior. To accomplish this objective, the cuts would generally run along a large area of flesh and then the skin would be peeled off from the top of the cut to the bottom. It is quite possible that St. Luke felt every nerve ending in his skin being ripped off his muscles as the flayer skillfully peeled off his epidermis. And undoubtedly, there were "thousands upon thousands of pain signals flooding [his] brain with each tug of the skin."[234]

Depending on the skill of the flayer, it was possible for the entirety of skin to be removed from the body without causing death, but rather, a long, intense agony that could go on for days. Death would eventually come from either exsanguination, infection, or hypothermia. Regardless of the actual cause of death, the intense agony probably lasted for several hours or days.

The Apostles, as was mentioned, knew Jesus. They spent every moment of three years with Him. They witnessed His presence after He rose from the dead. They ate with Him, placed their fingers in His wounds, and saw Him ascend into heaven. They knew He was God. Their first-hand witness accounts also served to convince many who came after them of Jesus's true divinity. It is doubtful that anyone would have been willing to subject themselves to the type of pain they endured for a person, or cause, they knew to be fraudulent. Rather, knowing that Jesus is God and that He resurrected from the dead following His sacrificial crucifixion was enough to change everything for them and for all the early Christians who believed them.

After the initial twelve Apostles and that first generation of Christian faithful were gone, Christians continued to risk their lives for the cause, despite not having seen Jesus in person or knowing anyone who had. Yet they persevered. Though the practice of Christianity was illegal and punishable by torturous deaths, they did not close their "churches," but rather chose to continue to meet and celebrate the "Mass" even if they did so underground and in catacombs. They risked a similarly torturous death each time they met in secret celebration of the Mass.

This example of selfless ministering was continued throughout the ages regardless of the certain danger to health and safety. From 1873 to 1884, Saint Damien of Molokai lived in a leper colony among the lepers he cared for. He didn't worry about contracting leprosy because he believed he had a priestly obligation to minister to those who had no one. He did eventually contract and die from the disease, but clearly, fear did not prevent him from doing his job.

Saint Mother Teresa of Calcutta, likewise, subjected herself to all sorts of disease to demonstrate the charity of Jesus to those who had no one. The Missionaries of Charity, a religious order she founded in 1947, managed homes for people who were dying of HIV and AIDS, tuberculosis, and leprosy. "They ran soup kitchens, mobile clinics, family counselling programs, orphanages, schools, and dispensaries. In addition to the order's vows of chastity, poverty, and obedience, they also professed a fourth vow – to give 'wholehearted free service to the poorest of the poor.'"[235] Mother Teresa and her Missionaries of Charity did not worry about the impact to their own health, but rather only the effect on those they treated and served.

And of course, the same is true of the Catholic priests of Dachau, who risked "hunger, torture, medical experimentation and mass executions,"[236] to sneak the Eucharist into the concentration camp, provide it to the prisoners, and minister the other sacraments to them.

"One Catholic deacon was even ordained to the priesthood while in captivity. [Dachau] was the largest religious community living together in the history of the Catholic Church and these were priests who lived their faith and their vocations with heartbreaking focus and love, and who were determined to build the body of Christ."[237]

Dianne Traflet, Assistant Professor of Pastoral Theology and Associate Dean of Graduate Studies at Seton Hall University addressed a conference of permanent deacons and their families on July 24, 2018. She "spoke of how priests donated blood, volunteered to serve in Dachau's deadly typhus ward and surreptitiously celebrated Mass using smuggled consecrated hosts."[238]

Catholic priests were not the only people who risked their own safety to promote their faith. The life of Franz Jägerstätter provides another World War II example of having courage of conviction in the face of certain death.

Jägerstätter was called to service as a Nazi soldier but refused to serve on the grounds that the principles for which Germany was fighting violated his Catholic faith. In 1938 he openly opposed the German annexation of Austria and was subsequently drafted into the Austrian Army where, after training for seven months, he was given a deferment. In 1940 he was again called up but was allowed to return home after the intervention of the mayor of his hometown. He was called into active service for a third time between October 1940 and April 1941, but again received a deferment, despite the urging of his pastor, other priests, and the bishop of Linz, who all advised him not to refuse to serve if drafted. In February of 1943 he was called up for service a fourth time and reported to army officials in Enns, Austria. Once there, however, "he refused to take the oath of loyalty to Hitler"[239] and was imprisoned. His subsequent offer to serve in the medical corps was rejected, and Jägerstätter feared for the worse.

During Holy Week of that year, he wrote a letter to his wife: "Easter is coming and, if it should be God's will that we can never again in this world celebrate Easter together in our intimate family circle, we can still look ahead in the happy confidence that, when the eternal Easter morning dawns, no one in our family circle shall be missing – so we can then be permitted to rejoice together forever."[240] Just a few weeks later, Jägerstätter was transferred to a prison in Berlin.

His attorney tried to reason with him noting that many Catholics were serving in the army. Unwavering, Jägerstätter replied, "I can only act on my own conscience. I do not judge anyone. I can only judge myself. I have considered my family. I have prayed and put myself and my family in God's hands. I know that, if I do what I think God wants me to do, he will take care of my family."

On the eighth of August, perhaps sensing the end, he penned another letter to his wife. "Dear wife and mother," he wrote, "I thank you once more from my heart for everything that you have done for me in my lifetime, for all the sacrifices that you have borne for me. I beg you to forgive me if I have hurt or offended you, just as I have forgiven everything...My heartfelt greetings for my dear children. I will surely beg the dear God, if I am permitted to enter heaven soon, that he will set aside a little place in heaven for all of you."[241]

The following day, Franz Jägerstätter was beheaded. He was beatified in Linz on October 26, 2007.

Shortly after World War II Satan's hold began to tighten. How far the faith has plunged since then. In the twenty-first century the Catholic Church faces a worldwide apostasy among the faithful, some bishops and other Church leaders. In parts of the world, such as Germany, the apostasy threatens to morph into another schism within the Church.

This may all sound a bit conspiratorial, but today there are things going on in the world, and right here in the United States, about which the casual observer may know nothing. For example, there is a town in the United States that opens its council meetings with a prayer to Lucifer.

> *"When the local government of Kenai Borough decided to welcome other faiths to their assemblies, they probably didn't envision opening up their doors to the Lord of Darkness....Iris Fontana, reportedly a member of the Satanic Temple organization that views Satan as a symbol for rebellion and rational inquiry – gave the assembly invocation usually reserved for pastors....Assembly members stood silently in a circle while Fontana asked them to 'embrace the Luciferian impulse to eat of the tree of knowledge. Then ended the surreal prayer with the words, 'Hail Satan.'"[242]*

Emboldened by their secular success in government, the Satanic Temple "rolled out extra-curricular clubs across the United States. 'After School Satan' is the Temple's response to a Supreme Court ruling allowing evangelical religious programs to operate in schools."[243] Nine clubs opened for business in Los Angeles, Salt Lake City, and Washington, D.C.

> *In a more recent atrocity, a proposed California "ethnic studies program urges students to chant to the Aztec deity of human sacrifice. [The] studies' curriculum advocates for the 'decolonization' of American society and elevates Aztec religious symbolism – all in the service of left-wing political ideology.... the new program, called the Ethnic Studies Model Curriculum, seeks to extend the Left's cultural dominance of California's public university system, 50 years in the making, to the state's entire primary and secondary education system, which consists*

of 10,000 public schools serving a total of 6 million students."

The California proposal is based on a theory by Paolo Freire, a Marxist theoretician, the 'pedagogy of the oppressed,' which asserts,

"Students must be educated about their oppression in order to attain 'critical consciousness' and, consequently develop the capacity to overthrow their oppressors. ...The model curriculum instructs teachers to help students 'challenge racism and other forms of power and imperialist/colonial beliefs, and critique 'white supremacy, racism and other forms of power and oppression."[244]

The final vote to adopt the proposal into the curriculum came on Thursday, March 18, 2021 after "four drafts and 100,000 public comments." Passage was hailed by former state legislator Luis Alejo, author of the legislation, who said, "In a state with the most diverse student body of anywhere in the nation, our students must see themselves reflected in their school, their curriculum, and the knowledge they learn...This first-in-the-nation model curriculum will show other states what is possible."[245]

As told at Fatima, this apostasy even extends into the Catholic Church reaching to the highest levels of the priesthood. Today's Catholic Church includes priests who promote LGBT church marriages in open defiance of the Vatican's prohibition on blessing same-sex unions. In Germany, Rev. James Martin, has lent his support to this cause. He quoted Father Jan Korditschke, a Jesuit who led same-sex couples at a worship service in May 2021. Korditschke said,

"I am convinced that homosexual orientation is not bad, nor is homosexual love a sin. I want to celebrate the love of homosexuals with these blessings because the love of homosexuals is something good."[246]

There are Catholic priests throughout the world who encourage giving Holy Communion to elected officials who openly support the killing of babies in the mother's womb, a process euphemistically referred to as a "woman's right to choose," or worse, "health care." It is an issue that is splitting the Catholic Conference of Bishops to such an extent that the pope felt it necessary to intervene, according to a recent report by the Associated Press.

Bishops hold differing opinions and attitudes on the rules for withholding Holy Communion from Catholics. One school of thought suggests that Holy Communion should not be given to a Catholic who openly supports and promotes the egregious sin of abortion. Others argue that it is up to the individual to excommunicate themselves. As the debate raged within the United States Catholic Conference of Bishops on whether or not elected officials who support and openly promote abortion should be denied the Eucharist, the Vatican's Congregation for the Doctrine of the Faith weighed in urging caution on the part of the bishops in their deliberation of this matter.

While some took that as the pope's call to deny the Eucharist to offending Catholics, others received quite the opposite message. The communication sent by the head of the Vatican's doctrine office to the U.S. Conference of Catholic Bishops simply urged them

> *"to carefully deliberate before making a decision on whether Catholic public figures — like President Biden — should be denied Communion if they support abortion rights. While the choice to deny Communion to individuals would be up to individual bishops, the issue has created major division within the Conference. Some members strongly support the measure, whereas others believe the move would be 'politically polarizing.'"*[247]

Rather than providing perspective on the issue, however, the message created more confusion. During a recent interview with U.S. House Speaker Nancy Pelosi, a pro-abortion Catholic, in which she was asked about the pope's intervention in the matter of pro-abortion Catholics being given Communion, a reporter noted, that the ultimate decision, would be up to the individual priests. Pelosi authoritatively answered,

"No. It [the Pope's intervention] basically said, 'Don't be divisive on the subject.' To Pelosi, neither the CDF nor the Vatican nor the pope nor her bishop nor her priest have the say on whether she receives communion. She does. She alone does. [She said,] 'I think I can use my own judgement on that.'"[248]

The assent by houses of worship to the government's demands in the war against Covid-19 provides another example of the apostasy as it contrasts not only the tenacity of Christians, who didn't hesitate to give their lives for the cause, but with the words of Jesus who, between 1931 and 1939, appeared many times to Saint Faustina Kowalska, and told her, "Do not be afraid of what will happen to you. I will give you nothing beyond your strength. You know the power of My grace; let that be enough."[249] The promise of Jesus to Saint Faustina in conversations determined by the Catholic Church to be worthy of belief, is also true for each of us. Jesus will give no one more than their ability to handle.

Despite the acquiescence of some, many Church leaders did protest and speak out. After Catholic Governor Andrew Cuomo imposed harsher restrictions on churches than on any other type of business in New York, the Roman Catholic Diocese of New York, Brooklyn, took the governor to court. Despite a series of lower-court judicial wins, the governor continued his discriminatory practices against churches in the state, issuing Executive Order 202.68 (EO) that prohibited gatherings in houses of worship in excess of ten persons or less if the building was located in a designated "red zone," a reference to a color-coded system used to determine the severity of Covid-19-related cases. The case wound its way to the U.S. Supreme Court, which ruled on November 26, 2020, that "the EO unfairly applied gathering restrictions to houses of worship by significantly reducing the allowed gathering size to 10 persons while other businesses, including liquor stores and acupuncture clinics, were not so fiercely regulated."[250]

Another American prelate of the Roman Catholic Church who led the charge against government's intervention in Church matters in the United States was Salvatore Joseph Cordileone, Archbishop of San Francisco, California. Described as a traditional theologian known for his willingness to celebrate Mass in the Extraordinary Form of the Roman Rite, Cordileone resisted the government's effort to unreasonably interfere with church services once he discovered that the restrictions imposed were both excessive and punitive, going far beyond those restrictions applied to other businesses.

California Governor Gavin Newsom has been described as "'the worst governor in America' for religious freedom."[251] Newsom began a lockdown of all nonessential businesses in California on March 19, 2020, allowing only those businesses deemed essential to remain open. The list of essential businesses did not include churches, however. After remaining completely closed for more than two months, Newsom finally allowed churches to reopen on May 26, 2020, but at a limited capacity of 25 percent and with a cap of 99 people. In some large churches that is less than one person per pew. Even this action was rolled back just a couple of months later, however, when an additional lockdown was imposed. It lasted until April 8, 2021 for most of the state. On that date a color-coded tier system allowing limited societal openings was implemented, though it was almost impossible to meet. During that time, Newsom also imposed additional restrictions on churches that impeded or banned singing in church, outdoor church services, and Bible studies.

Harvest Rock Church of Pasadena, California, took the protest to a higher level by remaining open throughout the pandemic. "Pastor [Ché Ahn] and his parishioners were threatened with daily criminal charges that were up to a year in prison."[252] Still, Ahn would not relent. He stood firm and took his case to court where on May 14, 2021, a federal judge ruled in favor of the Church, ordering Governor Newsom to "pay $1.35 million over the state's draconian lockdown of 3,000 churches during the coronavirus pandemic...The order told Newsom and all state officials to stop regulating church attendance unless a specific set of infection statistics occur, which is unlikely."[253]

The unquestioned acquiescence of some Church leaders to secular powers in the closing of the churches even stands in stark contrast to the courage of some of the world's political leaders of today who vigorously defend the faith and the Church teachings, even at the risk of imprisonment. The example of Finland's former Interior Minister and leader of the Christian Democrats is a case in point. In 2019, Interior Minister Päivi Räsänen was criminally charged for posting a picture of the

Bible, opened to Romans 1:24-27, after she became disturbed by the Evangelical Lutheran Church joining a gay pride event. The photo was a means of reminding the Church leaders of what God had to say about homosexuality. Her actions led to a two-year investigation, three police interrogations, and a criminal charge of hate speech. Because Räsänen had always defended and respected both the human dignity and the human rights of homosexuals, the charge took her by surprise. Räsänen said,

> *"A conviction based on the Christian faith is more than a surficial opinion. The early Christians did not renounce their faith in lions' caves; why should I then renounce my faith in the court room? I will not step back from my conviction nor from my writings. I do not apologize for the writings of the Apostle Paul either. I am ready to defend freedom of speech and religion as far as is necessary. The Apostle Paul's teaching is not only about defending marriage between man and woman, but about how a human being is saved into eternal life. If the teachings of God's word about sin are rejected, also the whole core of Christian faith is made empty – the precious sacrifice of Jesus on the cross for the sake of everyone's sins and the way He opened into eternity."[254]*

One does not have to travel to Helsinki to find this type of political courage in the face of anti-Christian persecution. In late February 2021, in the Congress of the United States, Rep. Greg Steube (R-FL) stood on the House floor and read about the differences between males and females from the Bible's Book of Deuteronomy. Rep. Jerrold Nadler (D-NY) chastised his colleague saying, "What any religious tradition describes as God's will is no concern of this Congress." Nadler's visceral reaction begs the question: How long will it take before the climate of hostility experienced in Finland reaches the shores of America? Or has it already arrived?

After years of telling Catholics how vital it is to receive the sacraments regularly and often, the unfortunate message conveyed to some Catholics by a very vocal minority in the Catholic Church through an acquiescence to anti-Catholic secularism was quite contrary to the actions of the early Christians or those of the faith leaders of the Catholic Church right up to the end of the twentieth century. The ability for a Catholic to receive the sacraments was put on hold for the perceived benefit of the public health. That message is even contrary to the actions of some of the world's current political leaders, who risk everything in the defense of the faith.

In 1917, Mary appeared at Fatima at a time when secular political influences threatened to abolish all religion within two generations. She warned the people of the world that if they did not amend their lives, sacrifice for the conversion of sinners and in reparation for offenses committed against God and Our Lady's Immaculate Heart, and if they did not pray the Rosary every day, the Church would suffer an apostasy that would nearly cripple it. She demonstrated the horrors of such an apostasy to the three children through a vision that is the essence of the hotly debated third secret.

Mary's depiction of the apostasy foretold at Fatima lends credence to the 1884 prophesy of Pope Leo XIII who overheard a conversation between God and Satan in which Satan told God that he could destroy the Church if given another hundred years and greater power. God granted the devil both requests. Many believe that the "century of Satan" began in 1917 with the advent of World War I. Looking at the events of the twentieth and twenty-first centuries, it is hard to argue against that possibility. One hundred years later, a vast minority of priests and bishops of the Catholic Church support abortion, champion transgenderism, perform Church wedding services between homosexual couples, bow to the wishes of secular authority who attempt to destroy the very foundation of our Catholic values, and were participants in sexual assault and the massive coverup that followed. And though those undermining the Church from within are a vast minority, they are a vocal and active minority that demonstrate that Our Lady's prediction of an apostasy within the Church has indeed come to pass.

Mary's appearances at Fatima, however, also provided the weapons needed for the world to combat and overcome this great apostasy and all the influences of Satan, namely, prayer, and sacrifice. Praying the rosary every day and making sacrifices regularly for the conversion of sinners and for reparation of sins against the Immaculate Heart of Mary is the prescription Our Lady offered. These are the ultimate weapons essential to warding off the enemies of Catholicism and their external and internal attacks. Without doubt, the future of our Church is in our hands. How will we respond?

Notes

[1] Bernard, Jean, Priestblock 25487: A Memoir of Dachau. (Editions Saint-Paul Luxembourg 2004), Translated by Deborah Lucas Schneider, (Maryland, Zaccheus Press 2007) Page 10.

[2] Zeller, Guillaume, The Priests Barracks: Dachau, 1938 – 1945, (San Francisco, Ignatius Press 2017) Page 72.

[3] Ibid.

[4] Ibid. Page 73

[5] Ibid.

[6] Ibid. Page 74.

[7] The Holocaust Encyclopedia, The United States Holocaust Memorial Museum, the United States' official memorial to the Holocaust. 100 Raoul Wallenberg Plaza SW, Washington DC, DC 20024-2126. https://encyclopedia.ushmm.org/content/en/map/german-territorial-losses-treaty-of-versailles-1919.

[8] Blakemore, Erin, Germany's World War I Dept Was So Crushing It Took 92 Years to Pay Off. June 27, 2019.   https://www.history.com/news/germany-world-war-i-debt-treaty-versailles .

[9] Blakemore, Erin, Germany's World War I Dept Was So Crushing It Took 92 Years to Pay Off. June 27, 2019.   https://www.history.com/news/germany-world-war-i-debt-treaty-versailles .

[10] Ibid.

[11] Ibid.

[12] Apocalypse WWII, Deliverance, Season 1 Episode 5. Directed by Daniel Costelle and Isabelle Clarke, narrated by Francois Arnaud.

[13] Ibid.

[14] Ibid.

[15] Wilde, Robert, Biography of Adolf Hitler, Leader of the Third Reich, May 15, 2019 update. https://www.thoughtco.com/adolf-hitler-biography-1221627. Page 1.

[16] Ibid. Page 2

[17] Ibid.

[18] Ibid. Page 3

[19] Ibid.

[20] Ibid.

[21] Ibid.

[22] Ibid.

23 Ibid.

24 Rosetti, Chris, How Hitler Tackled Unemployment and Revived Germany's Economy. National Vanguard, June 30, 2018. Quoting John Kenneth Galbraith, page 2. The National Vanguard source is the Institute for Historical Review. https://nationalvanguard.org/2018/06.how-hitler-tackled-unemployment-and-revived-germanys-economy/.

25 Ibid.

26 United States Holocaust Memorial Museum, Holocaust Encyclopedia, Nazi Camps, https://encyclopedia.ushmm.org/content/en/article/nazi-camps?series=10.

27 Ibid.

28 Editors, History.com, Dachau Concentration Camp, November 9, 2009 updated on January 27, 2020. Page 1. https://www.history.com/topics/world-war-ii/dachau.

29 Ibid.

30 Ibid.

31 The United States Holocaust Memorial Museum, The Holocaust Encyclopedia. Pages 1-4. https://encyclopedia.ushmm.org/content/en/article/antisemetic-legislation-1933-1939.

32 Editors, History.com, Dachau Concentration Camp, November 9, 2009 updated on January 27, 2020. https://www.history.com/topics/world-war-ii/dachau. Page 2.

33 Ibid.

34 Ibid.

35 Ibid. Page 3.

36 Holocaust Encyclopedia – The United States Holocaust Memorial Museum. Concentration Camps 1933-39. https://encyclopedia.ushmm.org/content/en/article/concentration-camps-1933-39.

37 Ibid.

38 Wikipedia, The Holocaust Trains, Page 2. https://en.wikipedia.org/wiki/Holocaust trains.

39 The New Republic, The harrowing First Report From Dachau Concentration Camp, in 1934. August 8, 1934. Page 2. https://newrepublic.com/article/119850/1934-report-dachau-concentration-camp.

40 Ibid.

41 Bernard, Fr. Jean, Priestblock 25487: A Memoir of Dachau. Zaccheus Press, Bethesda, Maryland, 2004. The US Holocaust Memorial Museum. https://www.kz-gedenkstaette-dachau.de/en/historical-site/virtual-tour/barracks/.

[42] Description of the barracks is taken from Dachau Concentration Camp Memorial Site, KZ-Gedenkstätte Dachau, Number 9 – Barracks. https://www.kz-gedenkstaette-dachau.de/en/historical-site/virtual-tour/barracks/.

[43] The New Republic, The harrowing First Report From Dachau Concentration Camp, in 1934. August 8, 1934. Page 2. https://newrepublic.com/article/119850/1934-report-dachau-concentration-camp.

[44] Ibid.

[45] Criminals were marked with green inverted triangles, political prisoners with red, "asocials" (including Roma, nonconformists, vagrants, and other groups) with black or—in the case of Roma in some camps—brown triangles. Homosexuals were identified with pink triangles and Jehovah's Witnesses with purple ones. Non-German prisoners were identified by the first letter of the German name for their home country, which was sewn onto their badge. The two triangles forming the Jewish star badge would both be yellow unless the Jewish prisoner was included in one of the other prisoner categories. A Jewish political prisoner, for example, would be identified with a yellow triangle beneath a red triangle.
The Nazis required Jews to wear the yellow Star of David not only in the camps but throughout most of occupied Europe.

[46] Ibid.

[47] Dachau Concentration Camp, Chronos Media History, a Youtube video interview with Josef Felder, 37:11. https://www.youtube.com/watch?app=desktop&v=FMEkEGaDK6g.

[48] Ibid.

[49] Dachau Concentration Camp, Chronos Media History, a Youtube video interview with Josef Felder, 37:11. https://www.youtube.com/watch?app=desktop&v=FMEkEGaDK6g.

[50] Ibid.

[51] Dillon, Christopher, Dachau & the SS: A Schooling in Violence. Oxford University Press, United Kingdom, 2015. Page 10.

[52] Ibid.

[53] The New Republic, The harrowing First Report From Dachau Concentration Camp, in 1934. August 8, 1934. Page 3. https://newrepublic.com/article/119850/1934-report-dachau-concentration-camp.

[54] Ibid. Pate 4.

[55] Ibid.

[56] Ibid. Page 5.

[57] Ibid.

[58] Ibid.

[59] Statement of Stanislav Kamechik (Zamecnik) regarding the Dachau Concentration Camp. Stanislav died on June 22, 2011 in Prague at the age of 88 years. As a 17-year-old, Stanislav joined the Czech resistance movement immediately after the invasion of the German Wehrmacht. When he attempted to leave the country, he was arrested and deported to Dachau in February 1941. From November 1941 onwards he worked in the infirmary. Risking his own life, he procured drugs for his dying comrades, hid prisoners who were supposed to be murdered and got a deep insight into the cruel medical experiments of the SS. Page 2. https://furtherglory.wordpress.com/tag/stanislav-zamecnik/.

[60] Ibid.

[61] Ibid. Page 1.

[62] Ibid.

[63] Ibid.

[64] Ibid.

[65] Ibid.

[66] Ibid. Page 1 and 2.

[67] Medvin, Marina, Town Hall, The Dogs of Dachau: Never-Before-Published Letter Reveals How Nazis Used Dogs for Torture. Page 2. https://townhall.com/columnists/marinamedvin/2020/10/14/the-dogs-of-dachau-neverbeforepublished-letter-reveals-how-nazis-used-dogs-for-torture-n2577973.

[68] The New Republic, The harrowing First Report From Dachau Concentration Camp, in 1934. August 8, 1934. Page 5. https://newrepublic.com/article/119850/1934-report-dachau-concentration-camp.

[69] Harris, Whitney R., Tyranny on Trial: The Evidence at Nuremberg. Southern Methodist University Press, Dallas, 1954. 1995 edition published by Barnes & Noble, Inc. Page 424.

[70] Ibid. Pages 424 and 425.

[71] Ibid. Page 425.

[72] Ibid. Pages 425 and 426.

[73] Ibid. Pages 426 and 427

[74] Ibid. Page 427.

[75] The New Republic, The harrowing First Report From Dachau Concentration Camp, in 1934. August 8, 1934. Page 5. https://newrepublic.com/article/119850/1934-report-dachau-concentration-camp. Page 2.

[76] Ibid. Page 428.

[77] Kogon, Eugen, Langbein, Hermann & Ruckerl, Adalbert, Editors, Nazi Mass Murder: A Documentary History of the Use of Poison Gas. Translated by Mary

Scott and Caroline Lloyd-Morris, Yale University Press, New Haven and Londaon, 1993. Pages 202 and 203.

[78] Ibid. Page 203.
[79] Ibid.
[80] Ibid. Page s 203 and 204.
[81] Dillon, Christopher, Dachau & the SS: A Schooling in Violence. The Oxford University Press, United Kingdom, 2015. Page 40.
[82] Ibid. Page 42.
[83] Ibid. Page 35.
[84] Ibid.
[85] Ibid.
[86] Jewish Virtual Library, A Project By AICE, Dachau Concentration Camp History & Overview: March 9, 1933 to April 29, 1945. https://encyclopedia.ushmm.org/content/en/animated-map/dachau-concentration-camp

[87] *"Bevölkerung nach Religionszugehörigkeit (1910–1939)"* (PDF). Band 6. Die Weimarer Republik 1918/19–1933 (in German). Deutsche Geschichte in Dokumenten und Bildern. Archived (PDF) from the original on 14 August 2017. Retrieved 22 January 2018.

[88] Zeller, Guillaume, The Priest Barracks: Dachau, 1938 – 1945. Ignatius Press, San Francisco, 2017. Pages 133-134.

[89] Ibid. Page 134.
[90] Wikipedia, Catholicism and the Third Reich. https://en.wikipedia.org/wiki/History_of_the_Catholic_Church_in_Germany.
[91] Ibid.
[92] Zeller, Guillaume, The Priest Barracks: Dachau, 1938 – 1945. Ignatius Press, San Francisco, 2017. Pages 134.

[93] Wikipedia, Catholicism and the Third Reich. https://en.wikipedia.org/wiki/History_of_the_Catholic_Church_in_Germany.

[94] Zeller, Guillaume, The Priest Barracks: Dachau, 1938 – 1945. Ignatius Press, San Francisco, 2017. Pages 39-40.

[95] Ibid. Page 40.
[96] Ibid.
[97] Ibid. Page 41.
[98] Ibid. Page 45.
[99] Ibid.
[100] Ibid. Page 46.
[101] Ibid. Page 46 – 47.

[102] Ibid.

[103] Source: Zeller, Guillaume, The Priest Barracks: Dachau, 1938 – 1945. Ignatius Press, San Francisco, 2017. Page 258, taken from Johann Neuhausler, Comment etait-ce Dachau? Humbles approaches de la verite (Dachau: Administration du monument expiatoire du Camp de concentration de Dachau, 5th edition, 1980).

[104] Clark, John, The Amazing Story of Maximilian Kolbe (and Why it Matters Now, More Than Ever). October 2, 2020, https://blog.magiscenter.com/blog/maximilian-kolbe-story. Page 1.

[105] Ibid. Page 2.

[106] Ibid. Page 3.

[107] Ibid.

[108] Ibid. Page 2.

[109] Ibid. Page 4.

[110] Bernard, Jean, Priestblock 25487: A Memoir of Dachau. Zaccheus Press, Saint-Paul, Luxembourg, 2004, translation copy 2007. Page 174.

[111] Ibid.

[112] Ibid. Pages 174-175.

[113] Ibid. Page 12.

[114] Ibid. Page 13.

[115] Ibid. Page 14.

[116] Ibid. Page 15.

[117] Ibid. Pages 16-17.

[118] Ibid. Page 18.

[119] Ibid. Page 19.

[120] Ibid.

[121] Ibid.

[122] Ibid. Pages 19 – 20.

[123] Ibid. Page 22.

[124] Ibid. Page 24.

[125] Ibid. Page 25.

[126] Ibid. Page 28.

[127] Ibid.

[128] Ibid. Page 30.

[129] Ibid. Page 35.

[130] Ibid. Pages 35 and 36.

[131] Ibid. Page 37.

[132] Ibid. Page 192.

[133] Ibid. Page 195.

[134] Zeller, Guillaume, The Priest Barracks: Dachau, 1938 – 1945. Ignatius Press, San Francisco, 2017. Page 182. Taken from Johann Neuhausler, Comment etait-

ce Dachau? Humbles approaches de la verite (Dachau: Administration du monument expiatoire du Camp de concentration de Dachau, 5th edition, 1980).

[135] Ibid. Page 172.

[136] Ibid. Page 182.

[137] Ibid. Pages 182 and 183.

[138] Ibid. Pages 174-175.

[139] Bernard, Jean, Priestblock 25487: A Memoir of Dachau. Zaccheus Press, Saint-Paul, Luxembourg, 2004, translation copy 2007.

[140] Zeller, Guillaume, The Priest Barracks: Dachau, 1938 – 1945. Ignatius Press, San Francisco, 2017. Page 180. Taken from Johann Neuhausler, Comment etait-ce Dachau? Humbles approaches de la verite (Dachau: Administration du monument expiatoire du Camp de concentration de Dachau, 5th edition, 1980).

[141] Ibid. Page 183.

[142] Ibid.

[143] Ibid. Page 185.

[144] Ibid.

[145] Ibid.

[146] Ibid. Page 188.

[147] Ibid. Page 189.

[148] Bernard, Jean, Priestblock 25487: A Memoir of Dachau. Zaccheus Press, Saint-Paul, Luxembourg, 2004, translation copy 2007.

[149] Zeller, Guillaume, The Priest Barracks: Dachau, 1938 – 1945. Ignatius Press, San Francisco, 2017. Page 42. Taken from Johann Neuhausler, Comment etait-ce Dachau? Humbles approaches de la verite (Dachau: Administration du monument expiatoire du Camp de concentration de Dachau, 5th edition, 1980).

[150] Ibid. Page 51.

[151] Ibid.

[152] Ibid. Pages 54.

[153] Ibid.

[154] Ibid. Page 57.

[155] Ibid.

[156] Ibid. Page 58.

[157] Ibid.

[158] Ibid. Page 66.

[159] Ibid. Page 69.

[160] Ibid.

[161] Ibid. Page 71.

[162] Ibid.

[163] Ibid.

[164] Ibid. Page 73.

[165] Ibid. Page79.
[166] Ibid.
[167] Ibid. Page 80.
[168] Ibid. Page 81.
[169] Ibid.
[170] Ibid.
[171] Ibid. Page 84.
[172] Ibid. Page 85.
[173] Ibid.
[174] Ibid.
[175] Ibid. Page 86.
[176] Ibid. Page 99.
[177] Ibid. Page 103.
[178] Ibid.
[179] Ibid. Page 113.
[180] Ibid. Page 115.
[181] Ibid. Page 124.
[182] Ibid.
[183] Ibid. Page 125.
[184] Ibid. Page 128.
[185] Ibid. Page 132.
[186] Ibid. Page 133.
[187] Ibid. Page 137.
[188] Ibid.
[189] Ibid. Page 138.
[190] Ibid. Page 139.
[191] Ibid. Page 143.
[192] Ibid.
[193] Ibid. Page 145
[194] Ibid. Page 147
[195] Ibid.
[196] Ibid. Page 150.
[197] Ibid. Page 153.
[198] Ibid. Page 155.
[199] Ibid. Page 156.
[200] Ibid. Page 157.
[201] Ibid. Pages 157 – 158.
[202] Ibid. Page 158.
[203] Ibid. Page 160.
[204] Ibid. Page 161.

[205] Ibid. Page 166.

[206] Ibid.

[207] Ibid. Page 170.

[208] Ibid.

[209] Bernard, Jean, Priestblock 25487: A Memoir of Dachau. (Editions Saint-Paul Luxembourg 2004), Translated by Deborah Lucas Schneider, (Maryland, Zaccheus Press 2007)

[210] Ibid. Page 203 and 204.

[211] Ibid. Pages 204 and 205.

[212] The United States Holocaust Memorial Museum, Liberation of Nazi Camps. Page 1. https://encyclopedia.ushmm.org/content/en/article/dachau.

[213] Ibid. Page 2.

[214] Zeller, Guillaume, The Priest Barracks: Dachau, 1938 – 1945. Ignatius Press, San Francisco, 2017. Page 205. Taken from Johann Neuhausler, Comment etait-ce Dachau? Humbles approaches de la verite (Dachau: Administration du monument expiatoire du Camp de concentration de Dachau, 5th edition, 1980).

[215] Ibid. Page 206.

[216] Ibid. Page 208.

[217] Ibid. Page 202.

[218] The United States Holocaust Memorial Museum, Liberation of Nazi Camps. Pages 4-5. https://encyclopedia.ushmm.org/content/en/article/dachau.

[219] Ibid. Pages 209 and 210.

[220] Ibid. Page 212.

[221] Ibid.

[222] Ibid. Page 215.

[223] https://encyclopedia.ushm.org/content/en/article/polish-victims.

[224] Luxmoore, Jonathan, Catholic Priests, Nuns Were Among Those Killed by Nazis, Crux Magazine. May 10, 2020. Page 2. https://cruxnow.com/church-in-europe/2020/05/catholic-priests-nuns-were-among-those-killed-by-nazis/. [225] Ibid.

[226] Bible Gateway, New Living Translation, John 15:13. https://www.biblegateway.com/passage/?search=John%2015:13&version=NLT .

[227] Ibanez, Daniel, Archbishop Chaput: Some Catholic Bishops Were "Too Compliant" With Pandemic Restrictions. Catholic News Agency, June 3, 2021. Pages 1 & 2. https://www.catholicnewsagency.com/news/247881/archbishop-chaput-some-catholic-bishops-were-too-compliant-with-pandemic-restrictions. [228] Ibid. Page 2. [229] Ibid.

230 Ibid. Page 4.

231 Worldometer, Coronavirus, https://www.worldometers.info/coronavirus/. Page Also, Wikipedia, Covid-19 Pandemic Death Rates by Country. https://en.wikipedia.org/wiki/COVID-19_pandemic_death_rates_by_country. Page 2.

232 Pope Benedict XVI, The Apostles: And Their Co-Workers. Our Sunday Visitor Publishing Division, Our Sunday Visitor, Inc. 2007. Page 63.

233 Ibid. Page 71.

234 The Infographics Show, Skinned Alive: Worst Ways to Die. Youtubecap T? YouTube video series. https://www.facebook.com/TheInfographicsShow/videos/675043793116042.

235 Wikipedia, Mother Teresa, https://en.wikipedia.org/wiki/Mother Teresa. Page 1.

236 Donze, Beth, Catholic News Service, Historian Says Faith Lived in Dachau Section Set Aside for Clergy. CatholicPhilly.com, August 6, 2018. https://catholicphilly.com/2018/08/news/national-news/historian-says-faith-lived-in-dachau-section-set-aside-for-clergy. Page 1.

237 Ibid.

238 Ibid.

239 Franciscan Media, Blessed Franz Jägerstätter, Saint of the Day, June 7, 2020. Pages 2 & 3. https://www.franciscanmedia.org/saint-of-the-day/blessed-franz-jagerstatter.

240 Ibid.

241 Ibid. Page 3.

242 Home USA News, 'Hail Satan': Alaskan Council Meeting Opens with Prayer to Lucifer, August 13, 2016. https://www.rt.com/usa/355799-satanic-temple-alaska-assembly/. Page 1.

243 Home USA News, Satanic Temple Rolls Out After-School Program for Kids. August 1, 2016. https://www.rt.com/usa/354146-satanic-temple-after-school/. Page 1.

244 Rufo, Christopher F., Revenge of the Gods, California's Proposed Ethnic Studies Curriculum Urges Students to Chant to the Aztec Deity of Human Sacrifice. March 10, 2021. https://christopherrufo.com/revenge-of-the-gods/. Page 1.

245 Agrawal, Nina, California approves ethnic studies curriculum for K-12 schools after years of debate, Los Angeles Times, March 18, 2021. https://www.latimes.com/california/story/2021-03-18/ethnic-studies-finally-approved-california-schools. Pages 1 and 2.

[246] Catholic Vote, Fr. James Martin Promotes Open LGBT Defiance of Vatican. May 10, 2021. https://catholicvote.org/fr-james-martin-promotes-open-lgbt-defiance-of-vatican/.

[247] Gonzalez, Oriana, Vatican Warns US Catholic Leaders Over Proposal to Deny Biden Communion. May 11, 2021. https://news.yahoo.com/vatican-warns-u-catholic-leaders-155505915.html. Page 1.

[248] Kengor, Paul, In Persona Pelosi, Crisis Magazine, May 18, 2021. https://www.crisismagazine.com/2021/in-persona-pelosi. Page 1.

[249] Kowalska, Saint Maria Faustina, Divine Mercy in My Soul, Diary. Congregation of Marians of the Immaculate Conception, Stockbridge, MA., 1987. Diary entry 1491. Pages 534 and 535.

[250] Reid, John Wesley, "Gorsuch Writes a Scathing Rebuke of Governor Cuomo's Covid Restrictions as Supreme Court Rules in Favor of Religious Liberty, Standing for Freedom Center, November 26, 2020, https://www.standingforfreedom.com/2020/11/26/gorsuch-writes-a-scathing-rebuke-of-gov-cuomos-covid-restrictions-as-supreme-court-rules-in-favor-of-religious-liberty/. Page 2.

[251] Richards, Tori, Newsome Ordered to Pay $1.35 Million for Covid-19 Church Discrimination, The Washington Examiner, May 26, 2021. https://www.washingtonexaminer.com/news/newsom-ordered-pay-millions-church-discrimination. Page 1.

[252] Ibid.

[253] Ibid.

[254] Perkins, Tony, Convicted for Conviction? Finnish Leader Faces Jail for Bible Quote. CNS News Daily Newsletter, May 4, 2021. https://www.cnsnews.com/commentary/tony-perkins/convicted-conviction-finnish-leader-faces-jail-bible-quote.

Bibliography

Books:

Bernard, Jean, Priestblock 25487: A Memoir of Dachau. (Editions Saint-Paul Luxembourg 2004), Translated by Deborah Lucas Schneider, (Maryland, Zaccheus Press 2007.)

Bible, The New American, Revised Edition, Large Print. Oxford University Press, Oxford, New York 2010.

"Bevölkerung nach Religionszugehörigkeit (1910–1939)" (PDF). Band 6. Die Weimarer Republik 1918/19–1933 (in German). Deutsche Geschichte in Dokumenten und Bildern. Archived (PDF) from the original on 14 August 2017. Retrieved 22 January 2018.

Caranci, Paul F., The Promise of Fatima: One Hundred Years of History, Mystery and Faith., Stillwater River Publications, Glocester, RI, 2017.

Cornwell, John, Hitler's Pope: The Secret History of Pius XII. Viking, the Penguin Group, New York, 1999.

Dillon, Christopher, Dachau & the SS: A Schooling in Violence. Oxford University Press, United Kingdom, 2015.

Harris, Whitney R., Tyranny on Trial: The Evidence at Nuremberg. Southern Methodist University Press, Dallas, 1954. 1995 edition published by Barnes & Noble, Inc.

Kowalska, Saint Maria Faustina, Divine Mercy in My Soul, Diary. Congregation of Marians of the Immaculate Conception, Stockbridge, MA, 1987.

Kogon, Eugen, Langbein, Hermann & Rückerl, Adalbert, Editors, Nazi Mass Murder: A Documentary History of the Use of Poison Gas. Translated by Mary Scott and Caroline Lloyd-Morris, Yale University Press, New Haven and London, 1993.

Pope Benedict XVI, The Apostles: And Their Co-Workers. Our Sunday Visitor Publishing Division, Our Sunday Visitor, Inc., 2007.

Zeller, Guillaume, The Priest Barracks: Dachau, 1938 – 1945. Ignatius Press, San Francisco, 2017. Taken from Johann Neuhausler, Comment etait-ce Dachau? Humbles approaches de la verite (Dachau: Administration du monument expiatoire du Camp de concentration de Dachau, 5th edition, 1980).

Reports:
Quinn, William W., Colonel G.S.C., Dachau. A C of S, G-2, 7th U.S. Army,
Report on the Liberation of Dachau. 1945.
https://www.jewishvirtuallibrary.org/jsource/Holocaust/Shaef/shaef_oss_Dacha
u_report.pdf.

Internet Sources:
Agrawal, Nina, California approves ethnic studies curriculum for K-12 schools
after years of debate, *Los Angeles Times*, March 18, 2021.
https://www.latimes.com/california/story/2021-03-18/ethnic-studies-finally-
approved-california-schools.

Bible Gateway, New Living Translation, John 15:13.
https://www.biblegateway.com/passage/?search=John%2015:13&version=NLT.

Blakemore, Erin, Germany's World War I Debt Was So Crushing It Took 92
Years to Pay Off. June 27, 2019.   https://www.history.com/news/germany-
world-war-i-debt-treaty-versailles.

Blaze TV Staff, Blaze Media, The Glenn Beck Program, The 'Most
TERRIFYING Story I Have EVER Had to Report': Glenn Beck Reveals Newly
Approved CA School Curriculum. March 30, 2021.
https://www.theblaze.com/shows/the-glenn-beck-program/california-schools-
chant-aztec?rebelltitem=1#rebelltitem1.

Bradsher, Greg, National Archives Prologue Magazine, The Nuremberg Laws:
Archives Receives Original Nazi Documents That 'Legalized' Persecution of
Jews. Winter 2010, Vol. 42, No. 4.
https://www.archives.gov/publications/prologue/2010/winter/nuremberg.html.

Bunson, Matthew, Catholic Martyrs of the Holocaust. CatholicMagazine.com,
Catholic Answers, November 1, 2008.
https://www.catholic.com/magazine/print-edition/catholic-martyrs-of-the-
holocaust.

Catholic Vote Newsfeed, Pro-LGBT Catholics at War With the Vatican, March
17, 2021, https://catholicvote.org/pro-lgbt-catholics-at-war-wth-the-vatican/.

ChurchPOP Editor, Exorcist, Catholics React to Rapper Lil Nas X's "Satan
Shoes" Containing Human Blood, March 29, 20201.
https://mail.google.com/mail/u/0/#search/churchpop+exorcist%2C+catholics/F
MfcgxwLtGqFfLfSsjnjHdMQCzWlbWxH.

Clark, John, The Amazing Story of Maximilian Kolbe (and Why It Matters
Now, More Than Ever), October 2, 2020. Blogpost.
https://blog.magiscenter.com/blog/maximilian-kolbe-story.

Connolly, Kate, *The Guardian*, Survivor Recalls Dachau, Where SS Terror Began 80 Years Ago. March 2013. https://www.theguardian.com/world/2013/mar/24/dachau-survivor-recalls-ss-terror.

Crowley, James, Newsweek, 5 Facts About St. Maximilian Kolbe, the Man Who Died For a Stranger at Auschwitz. August 14, 2020, https://www.msn.com/en-us/news/world/5-facts-aboutmaximilian-kolbe-the-man-who-died-for-a-stranger-at-auschwitz/ar-BB17XX1Y.

Dachau Concentration Camp Memorial Site, KZ-Gedenkstätte Dachau, Number 9 – Barracks. https://www.kz-gedenkstaette-dachau.de/en/historical-site/virtual-tour/barracks/.

Editors, History.com, Dachau Concentration Camp, November 9, 2009 updated on January 27, 2020. Page 1. https://www.history.com/topics/world-war-ii/dachau.
Franciscan Media, Blessed Franz Jägerstätter, Saint of the Day, June 7, 2020. Pages 2 & 3. https://www.franciscanmedia.org/saint-of-the-day/blessed-franz-jagerstatter.

Gajewski, Karol Jozef, Inside the Vatican, Catholic Education Resource Center, Nazi Policy and the Catholic Church. November 1999. https://www.catholiceducation.org/en/culture/history/nazi-policy-and-the-catholic-church.html.

Gonzalez, Oriana, Vatican Warns US Catholic Leaders Over Proposal to Deny Biden Communion. May 11, 2021. https://news.yahoo.com/vatican-warns-us-catholic-leaders-155505915.html.

Holocaust Encyclopedia, Liberation of Nazi Camps. https://encyclopedia.ushmm.org/content/en/article/liberation-of-nazi-camps.

Home USA News, "Hail Satan:" Alaskan Council Meeting Opens with Prayer to Lucifer. August 13, 2016. https://www.rt.com/usa/355799-satanic-temple-alaska-assembly/.

Home USA News, "Satanic Temple Rolls Out After-School Program for Kids." August 1, 2016. https://www.rt.com/usa/354146-satanic-temple-after-school/.

Ibanez, Daniel, Archbishop Chaput: Some Catholic Bishops Were "Too Compliant" With Pandemic Restrictions. Catholic News Agency, June 3, 2021. https://www.catholicnewsagency.com/news/247881/archbishop-chaput-some-catholic-bishops-were-too-compliant-with-pandemic-restrictions.

Jewish Virtual Library, A Project By AICE, Dachau Concentration Camp History & Overview: March 9, 1933 to April 29, 1945. https://encyclopedia.ushmm.org/content/en/animated-map/dachau-concentration-camp. Also, Concentration Camps: Timeline of Dachau, https://encyclopedia.ushmm.org/timeline-of-dachau.

Kengor, Paul, In Persona Pelosi, Crisis Magazine, May 18, 2021. https://www.crisismagazine.com/2021/in-persona-pelosi. Page 1.

Luxmoore, Jonathan, Catholic Priests, Nuns Were Among Those Killed By Nazis, CRUX Magazine, May 10, 2020. https://cruxnow.com/church-in-europe/2020/05/catholic-priests-nuns-were-among-those-killed-by-nazis/.

Medvin, Marina, Town Hall, The Dogs of Dachau: Never-Before-Published Letter Reveals How Nazis Used Dogs for Torture. https://townhall.com/columnists/marinamedvin/2020/10/14/the-dogs-of-dachau-neverbeforepublished-letter-reveals-how-nazis-used-dogs-for-torture-n2577973. Perkins, Tony, Convicted for Conviction? Finnish Leader Faces Jail for Bible Quote. CNS News Daily Newsletter, May 4, 2021. https://www.cnsnews.com/commentary/tony-perkins/convicted-conviction-finnish-leader-faces-jail-bible-quote.

Petrat, Gustav, Last Statement to the Court written while in Landsberg/Lech Prison while awaiting execution. Reprinted in Dachau Trials: Gustav Petrat Torture Accusations. November 1948. https://www.jewishvirtuallibrary.org/gustav-petrat-accusations.

Reid, John Wesley, "Gorsuch Writes a Scathing Rebuke of Governor Cuomo's Covid Restrictions as Supreme Court Rules in Favor of Religious Liberty, Standing for Freedom Center, November 26, 2020. https://www.standingforfreedom.com/2020/11/26/gorsuch-writes-a-scathing-rebuke-of-gov-cuomos-covid-restrictions-as-supreme-court-rules-in-favor-of-religious-liberty/.

Ridley, Louise, The Holocaust's Forgotten Victims: The 5 Million Non-Jewish People Killed By The Nazis, January 27, 2015, HuffPost UK. https://www.huffpost.com/entry/holocaust-non-jewish-victims_n_6555604.

Richards, Tori, Newsom Ordered to Pay $1.35 Million for Covid-19 Church Discrimination, The Washington Examiner, May 26, 2021. https://www.washingtonexaminer.com/news/newsom-ordered-pay-millions-church-discrimination.

Ritchie, Robert E., America Needs Fatima, Letter to members regarding public Satanism in town of Kenai, Alaska. February 3, 2021. See story by Charlotte Reformation, RC News, April 8, 2021, at https://reformationcharlotte.org/2021/04/08/city-council-meeting-in-alaska-begins-with-prayer-to-satan/.

Rosetti, Chris, How Hitler Tackled Unemployment and Revived Germany's Economy. National Vanguard, June 30, 2018. Quoting John Kenneth Galbraith, page 2. The National Vanguard source is the Institute for Historical Review. https://nationalvanguard.org/2018/06.how-hitler-tackled-unemployment-and-revived-germanys-economy/.

Rufo, Christopher F., Revenge of the Gods, California's Proposed Ethnic Studies Curriculum Urges Students to Chant to the Aztec Deity of Human Sacrifice. March 10, 2021. https://christopherrufo.com/revenge-of-the-gods/.

Schneible, Ann, Catholic News Agency, Heroism and Sacrifice: The Catholic History of Auschwitz, July 29, 2016 / 11:20 am America/Denver (CNA)

https://www.catholicnewsagency.com/news/34277/heroism-and-sacrifice. Statement of Stanislav Kamechik (Zamecnik) regarding the Dachau Concentration Camp. Stanislav died on June 22, 2011 in Prague at the age of 88 years. As a 17-year-old, Stanislav joined the Czech resistance movement immediately after the invasion of the German Wehrmacht. When he attempted to leave the country, he was arrested and deported to Dachau in February 1941. From November 1941 onwards he worked in the infirmary. Risking his own life, he procured drugs for his dying comrades, hid prisoners who were supposed to be murdered and got a deep insight into the cruel medical experiments of the SS. https://furtherglory.wordpress.com/tag/stanislav-zamecnik/.

The Holocaust Encyclopedia, The United States Holocaust Memorial Museum, the United States' official memorial to the Holocaust. 100 Raoul Wallenberg Plaza SW, Washington DC, 20024-2126. https://encyclopedia.ushmm.org/content/en/map/german-territorial-losses-treaty-of-versailles-1919.

The New Republic, The harrowing First Report From Dachau Concentration Camp, in 1934. August 8, 1934. Page 5. https://newrepublic.com/article/119850/1934-report-dachau-concentration-camp.

Wikipedia, Catholicism and the Third Reich. https://en.wikipedia.org/wiki/History_of_the_Catholic_Church_in_Germany.

Wikipedia, Covid-19 Pandemic Death Rates by Country. https://en.wikipedia.org/wiki/COVID-19_pandemic_death_rates_by_country.

Wikipedia, Mother Teresa, https://en.wikipedia.org/wiki/Mother_Teresa.

Wikipedia, The Holocaust Trains,
https://en.wikipedia.org/wiki/Holocaust_trains.

Wilde, Robert, Biography of Adolf Hitler, Leader of the Third Reich,
May 15, 2019 update. https://www.thoughtco.com/adolf-hitler-biography-1221627.

Worldometer, Coronavirus, https://www.worldometers.info/coronavirus/.
YouTube Video, Dachau Concentration Camp, Chronos Media History, a
YouTube video interview with Josef Felder, 37:11.
https://www.youtube.com/watch?app=desktop&v=FMEkEGaDK6g.

Historical Museums:
Holocaust Museum & Cohen Education Center, 975 Imperial Golf Course
Blvd., Naples, FL 34110. Phone number (239) 263-9200, Website:
https://hmcec.org/. https://www.yelp.com/biz/holocaust-museum-and-cohen-education-center-naples.

United States Holocaust Memorial Museum, Holocaust Encyclopedia,
Nazi Camps, https://encyclopedia.ushmm.org/content/en/article/nazi-camps?series=10.

Movies and Documentaries:
Apocalypse WWII, Deliverance, Season 1 Episode 5. Directed by Daniel
Costelle and Isabelle Clarke, narrated by Francois Arnaud.
The Ninth Day: A Film by Volker Schlondorff. Volker Schlondorff, Director,
Dachau Concentration Camp, Chronos Media History.

About the Author

Paul F. Caranci is a third-generation resident of North Providence and has been a student of history for many years. Paul served as Rhode Island's Deputy Secretary of State from 2007 to 2015 and was elected to the North Providence Town Council where he served from 1994 to 2010. He has a BA in political science from Providence College and is working toward an MPA from Roger Williams University.

Together with his wife, Margie, he founded the Municipal Heritage Group in 2009. He is an incorporating member of the Association of Rhode Island Authors (ARIA) and a member of the board of the RI Publications Society. He also served on the Board of Directors of the Heritage Harbor Museum and the Rhode Island Heritage Hall of Fame. He is past Chairman of the Diabetes Foundation of Rhode Island (formerly the American Diabetes Association, Rhode Island Affiliate) where he served on the Board for more than 15 years.

During his tenure on the North Providence Town Council, Paul's efforts earned him several awards. For his legislative work in the prevention of youth addiction to tobacco, Paul was recognized with the James Carney Public Health Award from the RI Department of Health and an Advocacy Award from the American Cancer Society. Paul's legislation to expand health care coverage to include the equipment, supplies, and education necessary for the home management of diabetes and his work toward the elimination of the pre-existing condition clause from health insurance policies written in Rhode Island were recognized with an Advocate of the Year Award from the Diabetes Foundation of RI and an Advocacy Award from the American Diabetes Association. Those new laws also made Rhode Island the first state in the nation to both eliminate the pre-existing condition clause and expand coverage for diabetes care. His efforts in exposing political corruption in his hometown earned him the Margaret Chase Smith Award for Political Courage from the National Association of Secretaries of State, the group's highest honor.

Paul is the author of thirteen published books including four award-winning books. *The Hanging & Redemption of John Gordon: The True Story of Rhode Island's Last Execution* (The History Press, 2013) was voted one of the top five nonfiction books of 2013 by the *Providence Journal. Scoundrels: Defining Corruption Through Tales of Political Intrigue in Rhode Island* (Stillwater River Publications, 2016) was the winner of the 2016 Dorry Award as the nonfiction book of the year. *The Promise of Fatima: One Hundred Years of History, Mystery, and Faith* (Stillwater River Publications, 2017) earned Paul a spot as a finalist in the International Book Awards, and *I Am the Immaculate Conception: The Story of*

Bernadette of Lourdes, (Stillwater River Publications, 2019) landed Paul the same honor. Paul's memoir, *Wired: A Shocking True Story of Political Corruption and the FBI Informant Who Risked Everything to Expose It* (Stillwater River Publications, 2017) tells his own story of courage in the face of the political corruption that surrounded him.

Paul and his wife, Margie, recently celebrated their 44th wedding anniversary. The couple have two adult children, Heather and Matthew; and four grandchildren, Matthew, Jacob, Vincent, and Casey. They continue to make their residence in the Town of North Providence.

Also By the Author

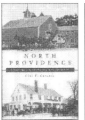

The History Press
2012

The History Press
2012
Named one of top 5
non-fiction books
of the year

Stillwater River Publications
2014

Stillwater River Publications
2014

Stillwater River Publications
2015

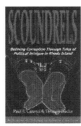

Stillwater River Publications
2016
Dorry Award
Non-fiction Book

Stillwater River Publications
2017

Stillwater River Publications
2017
Finalist in the 2018
International Book
Awards

Stillwater River Publications
2019
Finalist in the 2019
International
Book Awards

Stillwater River Publications
2019

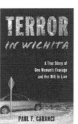

Stillwater River Publications
2020

Stillwater River Publications
2020

ORDER FORM

Please use the following to order additional copies of:

1. Darkness at Dachau: The True Story of Father Jean Bernard **($20.00)**
2. Before the End of the Age **($20.00)**
3. Heavenly Portrait: The Miraculous Image of Our Lady of Guadalupe **($20.00)**
4. I Am the Immaculate Conception: The Story of St. Bernadette And Her Apparitions At Lourdes **($20.00)**
5. The Promise of Fatima: One Hundred Years of History, Mystery & Faith **($20.00)**
6. Terror in Wichita: A True Story of One Woman's Courage and Her Will to Live **($12.95)**
7. Wired: A Shocking True Story of Political Corruption and the FBI Informant Who Risked Everything to Expose It **($23.00)**
8. Scoundrels: Defining Political Corruption Through Tales of Political Intrigue in Rhode Island **($20.00)**
9. Monumental Providence: Legends of History in Sculpture, Statuary, Monuments and Memorials **($20.00)**
10. The Essential Guide to Running for Local Office **($15.00)**
11. The Hanging & Redemption of John Gordon: The True Story of Rhode Island's Last Execution **($20.00)**
12. North Providence: A History & The People Who Shaped It **($20.00)**
13. Award Winning Real Estate in a Depressed or Declining Market **($10.00)**

___ (QTY) _____(Title) X ____ (Price) = $ _____

___ (QTY) _____(Title) X ____ (Price) = $ _____

___ (QTY) _____(Title) X ____ (Price) = $ _____

___ (QTY) _____(Title) X ____ (Price) = $ _____

___ (QTY) _____(Title) X ____ (Price) = $ _____

Total for books $_____ + Postage** $_____ = **TOTAL COST** $_____

**Postage: Please add $3.00 for the first book and $1.50 for each additional book ordered.

Payment Method:

___ Personal Check Enclosed (Payable to **M. Caranci Books**)

___ Charge my Credit Card

Name:_____ BILLING ZIP CODE:_____

Visa_____ Master Card_____

Card Number:_____ EXP:___/__CSC (3 digit code) _____

Signature:_____

(Order form continues on next page)

Ship My Book To:

Name _____

Street _____

City_____State:_____Zip:_____

Phone _____Email:_____

Special Signing Instructions: i.e. To Whom do you want the book signed? Do you want me to include a message? Just sign my name? Etc.

_____
_____

_____

MAIL YOUR COMPLETED FORM TO:
Paul F. Caranci
26 East Avenue
North Providence, RI 02911
You may also order using my Email address at municipalheritage@gmail.com
or by calling me at 401-639-4502
Please visit my Website at www.paulcaranci.com

Made in the USA
Middletown, DE
12 October 2022

12566948R00128